GETTING REAL ABOUT EDUCATION

In gratitude to two outstanding educators:
Patrick Power NT, and Fr Timothy O'Connor (1926-2005)

Thomas J. Norris

Getting Real about Education

the columba press

First published in 2006 by
the columba press
55A Spruce Avenue, Stillorgan Industrial Park,
Blackrock, Co Dublin

Cover by Bill Bolger
Origination by The Columba Press
Printed in Ireland by ColourBooks Ltd, Dublin

ISBN 1 85607 541 89

Acknowledgements
Chapter 1 was first published in *Oideas*, (Department of Education),
Earrach 1976, pp 5-15; Chapter Two was in *The Idea of a Catholic
University in Mayo*, Ballina 1996, privately printed, 35-45; Chapter 3 was
in *The Formation Journey of the Priest*, edited by Bede McGregor OP
Thomas Norris; Chapter 4 was first published in *The Sower*, and chapter
5 in *Irish Theological Quarterly*. The author gratefully acknowledges the
permission of the editors to reproduce these here.

Table of Contents

Preface: The Logic of Education Today   7

Chapter One: Education: What Direction?   19

Chapter Two: A Liberal Education for the
    Twenty-First Century: Cardinal Newman   33

Chapter Three: Understanding Faith   53

Chapter Four: Education of Catholics for Mission
    according to Cardinal Newman   68

Chapter Five: The Theological Formation of Seminarians   81

Index of Proper Names   101

The Logic of Education Today

One thing is quite certain: if you wish to know a person's or a people's treasure, look at what engages them most. Whatever it is that engrosses them most that is what they love most. It is not what a person or even a people says is important that is necessarily so. Rather, the important is what a people pursues in the planning of life, the choosing of work and profession, the selecting of goals, the making of sacrifices. For where a people's heart is, there also is their treasure. What people do influences us more than what they say. That is why we tend to prefer witnesses to teachers: if we listen to teachers at all it is because they are first witnesses!

There is still a second way of discerning a people's treasure. It is the way of education. Look at what they teach. Look at why they teach that particular curriculum. And look at how they teach it. For teaching as a primary moment of education is the organised process by which any present generation strives to transmit to the upcoming generation its own legacy of knowledge and learning, of wisdom and practical abilities. As the very correlative of that teaching on the part of adult population there is the challenge and the opportunity of learning on the part of the youthful population. Thinking of that learning, a contemporary writer defines education 'as the itinerary which a subject (either an individual or a community) pursues with the help of one or more educators, moving toward a goal considered worthwhile both for the individual person and for humanity.'[1]

---

1. Chiara Lubich, 'Honorary Doctorate in Education Address to the Catholic Universiy of America' in *New Humanity Review*, 5, New York January 2001, 10.

Education, then, involves both a content and a method. Both of these, however, are but functions of whatever is considered worthwhile. A people will always make its educational system serve its own self-image and promote whatever it considers of greatest value for being, well-being and the future. That this is true as a matter of plain historical fact can be seen by a cursory glance at some samples from the pages of the history of education. The Schools of Sparta taught Spartans the art of warfare and the values of heroic endurance. The Schools of Athens, those of Socrates and Plato, challenged their pupils to ask the right questions in order to critique the received wisdom of pragmatic teachers who could teach only the technique of success but studiously avoided the questions of meaning and orientation. These 'lovers of wisdom' challenged those who taught the art of success and called it education.

Famously, Socrates provided three benchmarks or criteria to assist his young student-friends in finding the way of life: 'It is bad to suffer injustice; it is worse to perpetrate injustice; it is worst of all to perpetrate injustice and to get away with it.'[2] The Christian Schools of ancient Alexandria wished to inculcate the revealed wisdom they perceived as falling from heaven in the gospel because it fulfilled the wisdom that had grown up upon the earth. Theirs was the conviction that 'what falls down from heaven wants to grow up from the earth.'[3] The great Cathedral Schools of the thirteenth century set out to inspire the new generations of believers by the dialogue with the recently discovered philosophy of Aristotle. The Schools of the Soviet Union taught systematic atheism and required three hundred hours of Marxism-Leninism from all third level graduates.

Ideally, then, education should involve an expansion of mind, heart and technical skill on the part of the young generation as they enter and exit the schools designed for them by the adult population. For this to occur, however, the students must

2. See Plato, *Gorgias*, London 1975, 469-475.
3. Klaus Hemmerle, *Bruecken zum Credo*, Freiburg im Breisgau 1984, 18-20.

first welcome the curriculum for life proposed by their parents. Nothing is given until it is actually received. But when it is received, there follows the wholesome fruit of unity and the desire for unity. Education, in other words, is an organic process of giving, receiving and desiring unity as between the generations. When this process is disturbed, there is breakdown in unity and a resulting conflict between the generations. Once again, it is enough to look at the panorama of history to see some examples of such educational breakdown.

What direction should the educational enterprise as such choose? The question raises the great issue of the ends and purposes of education. These concerns, however, cannot be addressed independently of the question, what is human living for in the final analysis? Though education is a big word, a still larger word is the human person. Education in fact is of the person, for the person and by the person. History witnesses to the fact that human beings ask unavoidable questions about truth, goodness and meaning, questions that will disappear only when the sun ceases to shine and the earth ceases to rotate on its axis. Still, these questions are a set that points towards a still more radical question, the question, namely, who is the human being? I call this the anthropological principle of education. In its broadest formulation, it states that education is made for the person, not the person for education. In its more philosohical formulation, however, it has to address the question of humankind's origin, identity and destiny.

Education – what direction?
The first chapter of this meditation on education outlines an anthropology, for education is an activity that human beings do with and for other human beings. What they think a human being is will largely determine that activity. The anthopology proposed here derives from the three great matrices of Western experience. These are the Greek, the Hebrew and the Christian. In each of these one encounters an authentic reservoir of reality. While the Greek articulates the issue of 'the substance of man',

seeing in him a tension towards the very ground of existence, the Hebrew underlines his mysterious dignity as a 'You' before the Creator in whose image he is made. The human being is addressed by the Creator. The Christian matrix, finally, reveals his calling through the God who became flesh so that the person might participate in the very life of the God and Father of our Lord Jesus Christ.

The Second Vatican Council stated the anthropological principle in these words: 'The truth is that only in the mystery of the Incarnate Word does the mystery of man take on light.'[4] In the light of this anthropology, the opening chapter draws out the implications of this vision for the integral education of men and women. It does so in terms of key imperatives and ten stated aims. The first of these aims is the cultivation of wonder as 'the basic spring of human learning'. Is not wonder the original spring of all discovery and knowledge?

The chapter takes very seriously a kind of rationality that is utilitarian rather than investigative, calculative rather that wonder-driven. Of this rationality, Chiara Lubich has written, 'A skeptical and cold rationality, dealing with things without reaching them in their original depth, has replaced the loving understanding which was capable, rather, of grasping the truth and beauty of creation *at its root*, that is, in God who contains creation within himself and nurtures it with himself.'[5] Utilitarianism is now a pervasive climate. Leaving out of consideration the most human of questions concerning human origins, identity and destiny, this climate leads inexorably to what C. S. Lewis called 'the abolition of man.'[6] Accordingly, an education that is person-centred will have to propose itself and find its way in an often uncongenial and unwelcoming public square.

---

4. Second Vatican Council, The Pastoral Constitution on the Church in the Modern World *Gaudium et spes*, 22.
5. David L. Schindler, 'A Comprehensive Unity' in *New Humanity Review*, 5, New York, January 2001, 23.
6. C. S. Lewis, *The Abolition of Man*, London 1943.

A 'liberal education' in the Third Millennium

Perhaps the educational level that most exhibits the preferred orientation of educational theory and praxis is third level. The university, in fact, is the laboratory of the educational enterprise *par excellence*. The explosive development of science, industry and technology is mirrored in the explosion of faculties and departments now constituting the modern university. The natural sciences and the human sciences have enlarged the curriculum beyond recognition. No longer is physics, to take but one example, an appendage to philosophy bearing the label 'natural philosophy'. Rather, the boot is on the other foot, with philosophy and the humanities increasingly pressurised towards the margins.

The new disciplines feed their graduates into the worlds of business and industry to the extent that the university is widely perceived as a training ground for the workplace. In the words of a contemporary educationist, '… learners come to be regarded as important human resources in an international competitive market. The purposes of teaching, the content of learning and the experienced quality of learning become accordingly recast. Teaching itself becomes increasingly characterised as a set of skills: significantly, skills that can effectively be itemised and increasingly carried out by the electronic operations of "e-learning." Teaching as a human practice thus recedes in this perspective, or is nudged aside, from the frontiers of learning and its advancement.'[7] It is in this very context that the second chapter, 'A Liberal Education for the Twenty-first Century,' expounds unabashed the guiding vision of Cardinal Newman's *The Idea of a University*.

As a place professing to teach 'universal knowledge', the university aims at welcoming 'the plurality of truths offered by each legitimate academic discipline, but it does not back away from the difficult work of ordering these truths, and securing the natural limit of each discipline.'[8] A university must provide

---

7. Pádraig Hogan, 'Teaching and Learning as a Way of Life,' in *Journal of Philosophy of Education*, 37 (2003), 207-223; here 213.
8. John Henry Newman, *The Idea of a University*, Oxford 1976, 375.

a 'culture of mind' by the training of the intellect, for 'education is a big word: it is a preparation of the mind and the imparting of knowledge in proportion to that preparation.' An educated man or woman will be able to think clearly and communicate effect-ively. Such a person will know the boundaries of the sciences, and will be alert to the transgression of those same boundaries. Newman called this expansion and formation of mind a 'liberal education.'

If an area of knowledge is omitted from the full circle of uni-versity teaching and research, three consequences result: there is ignorance of the omitted area, deformation of the full circle of knowledge, and the usurpation by a neighbouring science of the place vacated. A topical instance, mentioned by Newman, is what occurs when ethics is omitted. Such an omission will invite medicine to forget that 'bodily health is not the only end of man, and the medical science is not the highest science of which he is the subject.'[9]

Liberal education, however, is still not enough. The reasons for Newman's contention are as clear as they are cogent. 'A "knowledge culture" that is exclusively such leaves out of the reackoning the values and the necessity of goodness and gen-erosity. The human being is in fact an image of infinity, being made in the image and the likeness of God, and being born with an insatiable hunger for communion with mystery, love, truth and beauty. To disconnect the education of the human being from the integral identity of the human being is to deform and not to educate. Such a person may have everything he or she needs, except a reason to live and a reason to die! If the university project is severed entirely from the moral and spiritual, then the weight of knowledge, scientific technique and technology will crush out of existence the springs of love that are in the world – the family, the community, the volunteers.'[10]

---

9. John Henry Newman, ibid, 508.
10. From my Homily at Mass marking the 150th Anniversary of the Foundation of the Catholic University, University Church, Dublin, November 2004; see Hans Urs von Balthasar, *Love alone the Way of Revelation*, New York 1963, 114-5.

In the West, particularly in Western Europe, Newman's vision for education faces daily challenge. The co-ordinates of faith and culture which Newman took for granted, though he had a clear realisation of the rising tide of opposition to Christian revelation and the religious view of life, are now overlooked if not discarded. Accordingly, the next chapter, 'Intellectual Formation: Understanding the Faith,' has to address, albeit most briefly, the development of Western culture over the ages, looking at its sources in revelation and philosophy. The symbiosis of Greek and Christian revelation, effected with special vigour and depth in the thirteenth century, the century of Aquinas, Bonaventure and Albert the Great, has been severed under the impact of the renaissance, the reformation and the enlightenment.

The seriousness of this hiatus of faith and culture in Europe deserves attention. Europe was the one and only continent fully evangelised from the sub-apostolic times. Even with the profound wound of the Great Eastern schism in 1054, and 'the tearing of the net' (Pope Benedict) five centuries later with Luther, Calvin and Zwingli, Europeans retained their faith in Christ, crucified and risen, as the common denominator of the continent. 'The rejection of Christ and, in particular, of his Paschal Mystery – the Cross and Resurrection – entered European thought in the late seventeenth and early eighteenth centuries, the era of the Enlightenment ... So-called 'Enlightened' European thought tried to dissociate itself from this God-Man ... and every effort was made to exclude him from the history of the continent.'[11] The upshot of this condition is that the proposed Constitution for the enlarged European Union omits all mention of Christianity.

Identifying the Lord in the midst of the Idols
This state of affairs, then, requires an education for all believers that would bring out the unheard-of newness of Christian revelation. There is no easy route to that noble goal, just as there is no easy access to the mystery of the God of Jesus Christ. Besides,

11. Pope John Paul II, *Memory and Identity*, London 2005, 109-110.

the public square has different priorities. Francis Bacon had to deal with these idols of the marketplace in his day, just as Alexander Solzhenitsyn encountered them in the Russia dominated by Marxist dogma and its gulags. It is enough to read the latter's *Cancer Ward* (chapter 31) to see how the distortion of reality diagnosed by the sixteenth century Englishman asserted itself in twentieth century Russia. Students who want to know and live authentically must understand the form of such historical deformation.

To that end, immersion in the Great Tradition is indispensable. 'Although there is always a dominant climate of ideological opinion, there is also present, even in our society, a large community of scholars who have not lost contact with reality.'[12] This provides witness and resource for teachers and their schools. Teachers in fact have to understand the character of our day, its philosophical roots and the witness of the great teachers of the great tradition. We would not be what we are now if we had not been what we were then. Among other things, that requires the vigorous reconnection of philosophy and theology, as also of theology and spirituality. The separation of the last two has been a more serious bloodletting for the Church than either the Great Eastern Schism or the Reformation.

Preparing the lay faithful for their Mission
Our times, then, call for lay faithful who will be able to live and express their faith in the great areas of human activity and enterprise that constitute contemporary society. The fourth chapter considers the education of Catholics for the mission that is theirs in the world. 'In all times the laity have been the measure of the Catholic spirit; they saved the Irish Church three centuries ago, and they betrayed the Church in England.'[12] John Henry Newman wrote these words in 1858 in an essay bearing the title, *On*

---

12. Eric Voegelin, 'Why philosphize?' in *Communio*, XXVIII (2001), 875-883, here 877.
13. John Henry Newman, *Lectures on the Present Position of Catholics in England*, London 1892, 391.

Consulting the Faithful in Matters of Doctrine. The education of the lay faithful for mission at the beginning of the third millennium is more vital than ever. Since Newman regarded education as his most congenial scene, chapter four presents his blueprint for the education and formation of the lay faithful he desired. More particularly, it expounds his thinking in relation to four imperatives that are vital for their mission in bringing the gospel to bear upon the great forces that make up the modern world and are the specific arena of their activity. Under the organising and uniting cipher of integrity, these imperatives address four expressions of education: that of conscience for moral and religious education, of holiness for education in the spirit of the gospel, of our understanding of the bases and principles of Catholicism for confidence and composure in the public square, and of formal learning for an authentic culture of the intellect.

Educating Shepherds for the new Millennium

The life of human beings is marked by suffering and pain, as much as it is marked by achievement and virtue. Worse still, human beings do wrong and are the agents of suffering and social disruption. These phenomena challenge all perspectives on education. In particular, there exists a logic of cynicism and of brokenness. A 'real world' is identified as a place where competition replaces solidarity, exploitation altruism, and selfishness generosity.

This scenario requires any sketch of Catholic education to identify its revealed and dependable foundations. Is there 'an idea stronger than any calamity?', asks the great Dostoyevsky.[14] Must not an education worthy of the name hold in tension what Newman called 'the greatness and littleness of human life', what Pascal called its 'grandeur' and its 'misère'? The elementary and essential core of Christian faith finds its focus here. The fifth chapter addresses this very question in terms of the eternal Love that became flesh in order 'to taste death for all mankind' (Heb 2:9) and to overcome death as 'the last of the enemies to be de-

---

14. Fyodor Dostoievsky, *Roskolnikov's Diary*, ed. Fülop-Miller 1928, 417.

stroyed' (1 Cor 15:26). Resurrected and glorified, that Love inspires the whole educational project powerfully. Christianity is 'total newness, the newness Christ brought in bringing himself who had been foretold.'[15] Christ shows that 'one has no right to renounce his nobility under the pretext of quenching its misery.'[16] This chapter begins with a phenomenology of love describing the sevenfold form of love which, like the seven colours of the rainbow, guide a truly Christian education.

Believers share their goods, both spiritual and material, since they are one in mind and one in heart (Acts 4:32). They also radiate the life and the goodness they have discovered as the overflow of the love of God flooding their hearts by the Holy Spirit given to them. (Rom 5:5) The witness of loving is the key to the apostolate. But, thirdly, this same love elevates the mind and the heart towards its very source: prayer and spirituality emerge as a further colour of that one love. Further, love creates and builds the family of believers: the world of recreation, sport and health come into view. In the fifth place, since love causes harmony and each person is a temple of the Holy Spirit (1 Cor 6:19), the aspect of dress and the decoration of homes are also an aspect of the one love. Is not God beauty even before he is truth and goodness? Then there is the fact that love makes those who love desirous of knowing the Beloved better. The reality of study comes into view. Wisdom, and not only knowledge, will be the outcome of such study. Finally, since love sets up living relationships between all those it touches, communications are of great importance.

This phenomenology of Love links both the thinking out and the living out of the faith. In that way, theology and spirituality nurture each other reciprocally. The destructive separation of mind and heart is overcome, while learning inspires daily concrete living.

---

15. St Irenaeus, *Against the Heresies*, IV, 34.
16. Henri de Lubac, *Theology in History*, San Francisco 1996, 49; see n 4.

In conclusion

Though written on various occasions and for even more varied situations, these essays attempt to address certain aspects of education. Perhaps it is more accurate to say that they propose certain principles for education. We will now name these principles. The first essay stresses the *'anthropology principle'*: what kind of life is worth living? The answer depends on our idea of the human person. Education is for the person, not the person for education. Anthropology thus determines the aims of education.

Since the human person enjoys a 'detached, disinterested and unrestricted desire to know' (Lonergan), knowledge relentlessly investigates all the sectors of reality. Education then has the task of studying and investigating all the segments of reality. This may be called the *'liberality principle.'* Associated in a particular way with Cardinal Newman, it provides the imperative guiding and governing the university as a place that teaches universal knowledge. Truly educated minds will have what might be described as a sense of the architecture of reality. They will be able to distinguish the various areas in order to unite them.

In our third chapter, the realm of reality opened up by divine revelation is the subject of study and the object of the effort to understand. Historically this yielded the subject of theology as faith, hope and charity seeking understanding. Though focusing specifically on the intellectual formation of candidates for the priesthood, our third chapter still develops the *'rationality principle'* that is operative in all the areas of reality, even in the world opened up by the revelation of boundless mystery. Such mystery will always surpass our ability to understand fully.

What we receive in education enables us to find our way in life and to earn our bread. It also equips us to contribute to the world and to society. What we have received we have received from others, from parents, teachers, geniuses, writers, discoverers, saints and heroes. Education thus inspires us to want to give, and giving enlarges our hearts and our humanity. Our fourth essay considers the education of Catholics for their human and God-given mission to 'bear fruit in plenty'. (Jn 15:5) Here is the *apostolic principle* of education. Since we have received freely, we are called to give freely.

Finally, there is the theme of the theological education of candidates for the priesthood. Our reflections here stress the need to bond thinking the faith with living the faith. 'The love of God made visible in Christ Jesus our Lord' (Rom 8:390) not only bonds theology and Christian living, it also sheds its warm light over the whole of life. As a beam of white light when passed through a prism emerges in its seven component colours, so too the light of the glorious love shining on the face of Christ (see 2 Cor 4:6) scatters its radiance over the seven sectors of daily living. Possessions and apostolate, spirituality and home, clothing, study and communications together constitute the core areas of human existence. They must also operate at the levels of both Christian and priestly existence. An authentic education of the ministers of the gospel of Christ ought to include them. The concluding chapter thus proposes an *'inclusivity principle'* for education.

CHAPTER ONE

Education: What Direction?

In the midst of the last World War, Sir Richard Livingstone wrote: 'The history of mankind might be described by a cynic as a series of splendid expeditions towards the wrong goal or towards no goal at all, led by men who have all the gifts of leadership except a sense of direction and every endowment for achieving their ends except a knowledge of ends worth achieving.'[1] Perhaps only a modern cynic would unqualifiedly accept this as a fair definition of modern education. But there is some truth in it. Jacques Maritain, writing at the same time as Livingstone, made a similar criticism of contemporary educational practice and theory: 'This supremacy of means over end, and the consequent collapse of all sure purpose and real efficiency seem to be the main reproach to contemporary education. The means are not bad. On the contrary, they are generally much better than those of the old pedagogy ... Hence the surprising weakness of education today, which proceeds from our attachment to the very perfection of our educational means and methods and our failure to bend them toward the end.'[2]

Clear educational objectives are essential for our country's welfare in the future. Unless we can meet the challenge of our times with a deepening perception of what we are trying to do in educating our young people, the embryonic Ireland of tomorrow, we are heading towards a blurring of our identity, the

1. R. Livingstone, *Education for a World Adrift*, London 1943, p 42; see also p xl: E. B. Castle, *Ancient Education and Today*, London 1961, p 204.
2. J. Maritain, *Education at the Crossroads*, London 1943, p 3. Consider the relative insignificance of the space allotted to education aims in W. O. Lester Smith, *Education: An Introductory Survey*, London 1973, pp 28-31, only three and a half pages out of 233!

weakening of our culture, the eclipse of our Christian faith, and the disorientation of our people.[3]

Anthropology

When considering what kind of life is worth living, and so when choosing what kind of education is worthy of human effort, one inevitably faces the question of man's nature, his concrete existence in the world, his origin and destiny. And though the resultant anthropologies clash all across the pages of history, still this much is certain: whatever the view of the human being in a particular social milieu or historical epoch, that view determines both the objectives and content of education.

What, then, is man? The question is as old as *homo sapiens*. Its very antiquity is a sharp pointer to that quality of the human being which sets him apart from all the rest of creation. The human being seeks to know who he is, his place in the universe and the purpose of his very being. Left alone an animal may fall asleep; but the human being begins to ask questions.

Fortunately this recurring question has received equally recurrent answering throughout history. The answers can be grouped in three strands: the Greek, the Hebrew and the Christian. Combined, these provide us with what Maritain chooses to call 'the Christian Idea of Man.'[4]

The Greeks saw man as an animal whose supreme dignity was his intellect. The perfection of man consisted in the full development of his intellectual powers and his aspirations towards beauty and goodness. And so the education of man would necessarily take cognisance of the nature of man and be guided by it. The aim of life for a Greek was 'to make oneself; to

3. R. S. Peters' 'Mental Health as an Educational Aim,' in T. H. B. Hollins, *Aims in Education*, London 1964,p 87.
4. T. H. B. Hollins splendidly establishes the correlation of John Dewey's educational theory and practice with his view of man in his article 'The Problem of Values and John Dewey,' in *Aims in Education*, op. cit., pp 91-107. See J. Maritain, *Education at the Crossroads*, pp 6-7. The question is being asked with greater insistence today: see *Church in the Modern World*, Documents of Second Vatican Council, Section 10.

produce from the original childish material, and from the imper-
fectly formed creature one may so easily remain, the man who is
fully a man, whose ideal proportions one can just perceive: such
is every man's life work, the one task worthy of a lifetime's devotion.' It was hardly surprising, then, that Plato 'built his system of education on a fundamental belief in truth, and on the
conquest of truth by rational knowledge.'[5]

Eric Voegelin devotes the third volume of his great work,
Order and History, to a consideration of the Greek achievement in
developing the philosophy of man.[6] He boldly claims that the
Greek classical philosophy, as represented by Plato and
Aristotle, clearly articulates the question of the 'substance of
man';[7] and this philosophy then proceeds to build up a whole
society on the resultant insights. Society was the macrocosm of
the microcosm that is man.

The Hebrew notion of man is, in its essence, a moral and religious one. This inevitably followed from Israel's history, unique
in all the world, of being a people chosen directly by God to be
the depository of his gifts to the world.[8] As a philosophy of man
it was not opposed to that of the Greeks. Rather was it complementary to it.

The Christian idea of man, finally, derived from the fulfilment of the Old Testament drama: God, the lover of Israel, became man 'in the fullness of time'. In Christ, the God-Man, every
other man received both a call to share in his divine Sonship and
a summons to leave behind sin and evil.[9] The Christian fact
henceforth stands at the centre of Western civilisation under
which the Greek and Hebrew conceptions of man are sub-
sumed. What the Greek notion had dimly perceived in terms of

---

5. H. I. Marrou, *A History of Education in Antiquity*, New York 1964, p 98,
see Plato, *The Laws*, Book 1 644 ff.
6. E. Voegelin, *Order and History*, III, Baton Rouge 1957.
7. Ibid., p 24; 'The Gospel and Culture,' *Jesus and Man's Hope*, Vol III,
Proceedings of the Pittsburg Festival on the Gospels, Pittsburg, 1971.
8. Genesis 12:1-20; 22:16-18; Exodus 13:1-10; 13:11-16; Deut 6:4-9; 11:13-
21; Jeremiah 31:1-34; Ezechiel 16; Amos 11:1-4; Isaiah 40-55.
9. John 1:13. Gal 4:47; Rom 8:15-17; Gal 4:5; Rom 8:31-39; Eph 1:3-10.

intellectual devotion to truth, goodness and beauty, and what the Hebrews were taught by their Law, by their prophets and by divine wisdom, were lifted into a human-divine synthesis called the incarnation.[10]

The Implications for the Human Person
A few reflections immediately follow.

First, man can no longer be in doubt about the sense or purpose of his existence. The sublime aims of Greek classical culture are not open to the charge of being mere aspirations to pie in the sky. Truth, goodness and beauty were anticipated in Greece; they became historical fact in Israel. Man is meaningful.

Next, man can be seen to have an unlimited capacity. In the words of Cardinal Newman, 'he has a depth within him unfathomable, an infinite abyss of existence!'[11]

Thirdly, man is weak and sinful, and this precisely in his unwillingness to be what he is. He is a combination of grandeur and misery. In this consists the paradox of man and the enigma of his story, enshrined in his history and in his culture.

Fourthly, this in no way means that men may not declare that man is absurd and without meaning. Such deculturation, to borrow a word from Voegelin, is in fact a dominant characteristic of our age.

Finally, though a scholar like Maritain may accept an antithesis between the Christian idea of man as I have defined it, and the scientific idea of man as developed since the time of Newton and Descartes, many contemporary thinkers do not accept such an opposition. Bernard Lonergan, for one, sets out from the procedures of modern science and mathematics to develop a whole philosophy, which is not only consonant with the Christian idea of man, but is also incorporative of the idea that has emerged through modern science and technology.

10. *The Church in the Modern World,* s 22. 'The Truth is that only in the mystery of the Incarnate Word does the mystery of man take on light.'
11. J. H. Newman, *Plain and Parochial Sermons,* Vol IV, London 1869, pp 82, 83; Compare St Augustine, *In Psalmos,* 50.

Lonergan is very conscious of the scientific and technological revolution effected in the recent centuries. It is an understatement to say that this revolution has profoundly changed man's self-awareness and worldview. For many, this change is regarded as a total break with the idea of man that has existed hitherto. The partisans of this view like to speak of the 'Christian idea of man,' which they consider obsolete, and the newer 'scientific idea of man,' which is the fruit of man's great scientific and technological advances. To such a mentality to speak of a Christian vision of man is to speak about the past, about what has been, and so to miss the point for today. It is understandable that this mentality would discard religion and faith as irrelevancies in the house that modern man is so busy constructing for himself.

In his great work, *Insight*, Lonergan examines what it is to be a man, a person, today. After over 700 pages he arrives at a vision of man which, he contends, fits and squares with the scientific and technological pursuits of man today, but also with the 'Christian idea of man.' And he works out his vision by starting with a detailed and elaborate investigation of what is happening in the very procedures and methods of science itself! Has he despoiled the Egyptians of their riches?[12]

It is as if Lonergan says to scientists: 'Attend to what you are doing in your very work. Notice the implications of your method. There is something extraordinary in the fact that you inquire into data, that you break through to an hypothetical understanding, which you then try to verify. Reflect upon what you are doing and you will discover that man is a being with a detached, disinterested and unrestricted desire to know; that such a desire manifests itself in inquiry that is both ongoing and structured. If you continue to reflect you will gradually discover that man is a being who seeks meaning, who is open to total

12. B. Lonergan, *Insight: An Essay on Human Understanding*, New York 1963. It is beyond the scope of this essay to expound his thought. In short, Lonergan considers human knowing in the fields of modern science and mathematics, and from this goes on to consider what one ought to do (ethics), what one may hope to become (natural theology), and finally, what one is (anthropology).

meaning, all meaning, all truth and beauty and love. Is it not true that only the fullness of truth and beauty and love will satisfy his appetite and hunger – the very hunger and appetite that makes science possible in the first place? Truth should never fear truth, only error which obscures it. What you do in science is possible in virtue of that *eros* of the mind which opens the person out to the Absolute, the totally Other, the Un-known, the Beyond who is nevertheless dimly felt as present and immanent. In the very activity that constitutes modern science, in the very mental operations that constitute your own science, are to be found the basic elements of your anthropology. And wonderful to relate, that anthropology squares with the so-called Christian idea!'

In the current debate in Ireland concerning the education of the nation, the anthropology of Lonergan is significant. If the atmosphere is thick with the dust of controversy about the proper orientation of our educational theory and practice, there is need for a shower of rain to clear the air and to improve our vision of essentials. A sound anthropology, such as that suggested by Lonergan, could be what is needed. Its great value lies in its ability to get us beyond the false 'either-or' approach in education. It reveals how fallacious it is to conceive the problem as a choice between a humanist or secular orientation on the one hand, and a Christian one on the other, as if a solid anthropology were not at once both Christian and humanist. 'The Word became flesh': what is truly human is henceforth Christian, and vice versa.

To conclude this section I might attempt a descriptive definition of man as a body-person, lodged in space and time but reaching out towards the infinite through the exercise of his conscious powers of knowing and loving, and called in Christ to divine Sonship even now and eternal enrapture with the Triune God hereafter. Through his body he enjoys a relationship with the world, and the animal kingdom; through his personality he enters into a free society with other men based on respect, truth and justice, and into communion with God through Christ in the Holy Spirit. Man is 'an horizon in which two worlds meet,' the world visible and the world invisible. Any attempt at educating him will have to keep his identity in mind.

The Implications for Teaching

If I am called upon to involve myself in the education of a fellow human being, I now have an apprehension of what – better, of whom – I am dealing with. I realise that he has to start out from nothing, with nothing realised, and he must, as it were, begin to make capital. He is emphatically self-made.

And so I may consider myself as a helper in his education. The journey he has to travel as he advances towards the fullness of his destiny is worthy of his reality: like himself, it is splendidly incalculable and supra-human. I realise that Pascal was right when he said that 'man is greater than man', and right in a very peculiar sense. In the face of every boy and girl before me there is mirrored the mystery of his or her origin, the potential for his or her itinerary through life and society, and the promise of a success, not only earthly, but above all transcendent. If the education I impart is to avoid the sin of stultifying such promise or the blasphemy of lack of reverence for the dynamic unfolding of the person within, I must be attentive to this mystery, alive to this potential, and alert to such promise.

And so I will realise that the primary factor in education will be the inner spirit and mind of the pupil, and only secondarily my own teaching activity. In the words of Sir Arthur Clutton-Brock, I realise that

> education ought to teach us how to be in love always and what to be in love with. The great things of history have been done by the great lovers, by the saints and men of science and artists; and the problem of civilisation is to give every man a chance of being a saint, a man of science, or an artist. But this problem cannot be attempted, much less solved, unless men desire to be saints, men of science, artists, and if they are to desire that consciously and continuously, they must be taught what it means to be these things.[13]

13. A. Clutton-Brock, *The Ultimate Belief,* p 123.

What I have been doing is working out an anthropology which will throw light on man's essential nature and highlight his relationships to God, to his fellow men in society, and to the material world. It follows that his education will consist in his full human awakening to this potential. Education is the acceleration of his learning process. It is the stimulating and liberating of all his powers of knowing, loving and doing in order to fit him for the fullest possible life here below and eternal life in heaven hereafter. A sublime objective indeed, but one appropriate, surely, to the inner nature of human personality.

The Aims of Education

At this juncture it is possible to indicate more precisely the aims of education. To do so I shall avail of certain categories supplied by Piagetian psychology and epistemology, as well as by Bernard Lonergan. It is always difficult to pin down what is richest and deepest in life. This is especially true of the growth of the pupil being educated. However, this task has been facilitated by the critical categories established by contemporary philosophy.

The human spirit is constituted as exigence and thirst. Wonder, as Aristotle rightly saw, is the basic spring of human learning. It is this wonder that accounts for the early enthusiasm displayed by the child in elementary school. It is this spiritual drive, rooted in the mysterious depths of the human personality, which operates the various levels of human activity. There immediately follows a *first* educational aim: detect, cultivate and deepen this faculty in pupils.

As a corollary to this, whatever tends to thwart, kill or deaden this eros of the spirit must be carefully avoided.

Next, the educational process will require that the teacher 'assist the student in the personal, creative discovery of the truth'.[14] The creative discovery of the truth does not close the way to further discovery. On the contrary, it but whets the enthusiasm of the pupil to search further, to wonder more, to raise

---

14. N. D. O'Donoghue, 'Education Versus Inoculation,' *Doctrine and Life* 2 (1970), p 69.

further questions, and to inquire more deeply. Such discovery is open, not closed. As a result it in no way stifles the inner dynamism of the personality. 'To seek in order to find, and to find in order to seek still more,' should be the objective of the teacher.

From experience, the pupil goes on to understanding, to the attempt to understand, to penetrate to the core of his experience. And once he has understood he attempts to test his insight by critical reflection and verification. As a result he arrives at the possession of truth. A *third* goal of education follows: that of helping the pupils to understand and to judge for themselves. The intellect needs truth as its very food and life. And so the young intellect should be gradually guided into the possession of truth, which is to become its native atmosphere. In fact, the whole climate of education should be one of love for truth. Truth is the function of the school and of education, and is their only justification.

How much this has been neglected today can be seen all around us. Education has been given pragmatic or sociological aims. Very often what counts is not truth but success.

Professor R. Hutchins lamented in 1940 that, 'today the young American comprehends the intellectual tradition of which he is part and in which he must live only by accident: for its scattered and disjointed fragments are strewn from one end of the campus to the other. Our University graduates have far more information and far less understanding than in the colonial period.'[15] Let it be recalled that this thought had already been expressed by Plato in his *Hippias Major*, in which he reports the following dialogue between Socrates and Hippias: 'Perhaps, Socrates, this distinction will escape our opponent. That may be so, Hippias, but, by the dog, it will not escape the man to whom above all others I should be ashamed to talk nonsense and use a great many words for the purpose of saying precisely nothing. Who is this man? Myself – Socrates, son of Sophroniscos: I could no more bring myself to make a single unverified assertion than

15. R. Hutchins, *Education for Freedom*, pp 25-26.

I could to believe that I knew something of which in fact I knew nothing.'[16]

Fourthly, and following upon the possession of truth, there arises the demand for consistency between knowledge and activity. Pupils must be helped to live their lives according to what they perceive as true and good and beautiful. What is aimed at here is moral interiority and inner consistency in the pupil. The pupil learns to 'do the truth in love'.

What should characterise this stage of education is the selection of a new touchstone for activity, for choice, for living, one which 'changes the criterion of one's decisions and choices from satisfactions to values,' values being those goals that are judged and understood as good and beautiful.[17]

What is achieved or aimed at here has been described as 'self-transcendence.' It is identical with that 'conquest of internal and spiritual freedom' to be achieved by the individual person, or, in other words, 'his liberation through knowledge and wisdom, good will, and love.'[18] Once the pupil reaches this stage he is master in his own house, though his mastery always remains precarious and under attack. There remains the tension between the self as transcending and the self as transcended.

Fifthly, the responsibility of the pupil for his own life must be gradually brought home to him. Having experienced moral conversion and having acquired self-transcendence he will realise that 'it is up to himself to decide what he is to make of himself.'[19]

This is the appropriate stage at which to highlight for him the balance between individual and society, personal rights and social obligation, individual conscience and common good, citizen and state.

Sixthly, it will be necessary to heighten the pupil's awareness of what is happening to him along the road towards self-development. He is moving from a state of childishness into new

16. Plato, *Hippias Major*, 298.
17. Bernard Lonergan, *Method in Theology*, London 1972, p 240.
18. *Insight*, pp 27-30; *Method in Theology*, pp 35, 41, 51, 104. J. Maritain, *Education at the Crossroads*, p 11.
19. B. Lonergan, *Collection*, London 1967, p 242.

worlds of truth, value, love and beauty through the exercise of his intelligence, reason, choice and responsibility. He has left the nursery behind. The limitless world of truth and value and good and beauty opens out before him. By entering these new domains he ought to become a new being.

Seventhly, as man's desire to know and love is unlimited, the fulfilment of it can only be the fullness of truth and the plenitude of love. Accordingly, the pupil can now be helped to the realisation that all authentic religion is being in love unconditionally with God, that all authentic humanism is deeply religious, and that 'being in love with God is an ultimate fulfilment of man's capacity for self-transcendence'. He can be led to appreciate how the wonder that makes the child ask 'why,' the curiosity that motivates the scientific inquiry, the urge that demands truth, the inner dynamism that attracts us to the beautiful, the good, the valuable and the lovable flow back ultimately into the source of all these. *'Tu nos fecisti ad Te, et inquietum est cor nostrum donec requiescat in Te.'*[20]

Eighthly, I should now aim at working out a harmony between liberal, vocational and technological education. This would require the establishment of principles and their application to the actual situation in the Ireland of today.

Human intelligence operates not only through the mind but also through the hands. Science, mechanics and technology are in no sense an inferior form of human activity, into which the less bright pupils are inevitably directed or channelled. This means that all through the years of education, mind and hands should be used. Pupils can thus be led to internalise and to integrate into their own personalities the fruits of mental intelligence, which constitute the humanities, and the products of applied intelligence, which are modern science and technology in all their ramifications. In both, of course, the emphasis will be on

---

20. Thus, for St Augustine, man is *'capax Dei'*; for St Thomas he is a *'naturale desiderium videndi Deum'*; for Newman he is 'an infinite abyss of existence'.

the leading of the pupils towards understanding, truth and the personal perception of value.

Such I consider to be the best way of obviating the danger inherent in the apparent clash of liberal with scientific or techno-logical education. It is not a question of choosing one or the other. Rather is it our duty at this point in human history to pre-pare the pupil for life in a scientific and technological age. This means that he ought to have the ability to think and behave in a manner appropriate to a well developed human person; and secondly, that he should possess a skill or specialisation with which he can earn his living and contribute to the progressive development of the world in which his lot is cast. If one chooses a purely liberal education, one may develop one's personality but find oneself without a place in the modern world. If one insists on an early specialisation and training one produces an efficient animal but at the awful cost of deforming the human personality; insects like ants and bees are splendidly efficient but do not share the high dignity of man.[21] The danger of such an utilitarian perversion of education is a very real one, especial-ly in our increasingly industrialised society.

In the *ninth* place, education will set out to renew and renov-ate society. Such renewal, however, will come from elements in society which have themselves been regenerated. For human soci-ety is the structured resultant of the truth, goodness, values, principles of individuals, or the lack thereof, as these are incar-nated in individuals or institutionalised in society's structures. Education must attempt a proper hominisation and Christi-fication of this society. And this it can do by realising that reform begins in the individual's heart, whence it spreads to others. Maritain puts the point in a nutshell: 'In order to reach comple-tion such a necessary reform (of society) must understand, too, that to be a good citizen and a man of civilisation what matters above all is the inner centre, the living source of personal con-

21. E. B. Castle, *Ancient Education and Today*, London 1961, p 204; M. V. Smyth, 'Education: where are we going?', *Doctrine and Life*, 5 (1971), p 244; J. Maritain, *Education at the Crossroads*, pp 12-14.

science in which originate idealism and generosity, the sense of law and the sense of friendship, respect for others, but at the same time deep-rooted independence with regard to common opinion.' An authentic human being who has been assisted to become such by the education he has received will tend to improve society by his way of thinking, living, and acting. And such a product is the only justification of an educational system worthy of the name. Well has it been said that the saints and the martyrs are the true educators of mankind.

John Stuart Mill defined education in terms of 'the culture which each generation purposely gives to those who are to be its successors, in order to qualify them for at least keeping up, and if possible for raising the level of improvement which has been attained.'[22] I would propose as my educational objective, both the preservation of our true culture and its appropriate development, using the term 'culture' in its classical and in its contemporary connotations. Classical culture viewed itself as normative, and so binding for all places and all times. Modern culture, however, is an empirical reality and consists of that particular set of truths, meanings, values, and beliefs that inform the living of a particular group. Today the culture of both kinds is under assault. The philosophy of nihilism and 'being-unto-death' of Sartre and, to a lesser degree, of Heidegger, is in the ascendant. It mingles with the intellectual currents of our age, and there hidden represents a subtle threat to the very meaning of man and his existence. A thorough education for our age, then, demands more than ever before the development of man as man, in order to awaken the human personality to its fullest possibilities in truth, goodness, love, creativity. And so the *tenth* aim I envisage for Irish education in our time will be the assisting of our young people to evaluate critically what is being thrown at them by the numerous hidden persuaders in the various media. In the words of J. Veale, education 'will be subversive. It will be this,

22. J. S. Mill, Inaugural address as Rector of St Andrew's University, 1867.

first, because the trained intelligence is the best defence against the sophistries and shibboleths of all the human powers that be.'

Secondly, to the extent that it is rooted in the Sermon on the Mount, it will stand for those values that invert the order of values the world calls order. It will invite from all officialdom the question of the Grand Inquisitor: 'Why have you come to disturb us, for you do disturb us?'[23] Such an education will be our safest defence against what I might call the 'Munich spirit', that spirit which drugs a people or whole population into accepting everything, however untruthful, worthless, evil, horrible, or inhuman, provided it does not silence the promptings of selfish purpose or of supine indifferentism. A good education today will aim at making everyone responsible for everyone.

23. J. Veale, 'The Christian School,' *Studies*, 4 (1970), p 395

CHAPTER TWO

A Liberal Education for the Twenty-First Century: Cardinal Newman

In composing *The Idea of a University* John Henry Newman was convinced that he had achieved a clear definition[1] of a university. Beginning such a momentous project – 'What an empire is in political history, such is a university in the sphere of philosophy and research'[2] – he needed absolutely to get his subject into the clearest possible view. He needed to be systematic and, as far as possible, to provide a 'proof'[3] of what he was going to do. Above all, he wanted to define the notion of a 'liberal education' since this was going to be central to the university enterprise.

His definition has distinct strands in its makeup. First of all, there is the strand of the product, the students who are the *raison d'etre* of the whole educational project advanced by the university. They should be people who have come to acquire 'the culture of mind'. This 'culture of mind' consists in 'the force, the steadiness, the comprehensiveness and the versatility of intellect, the command over our own powers, the instinctive just estimate of things as they pass before us, which sometimes is a natural gift, but commonly is not gained without much effort and the exercise of years'. Further, 'it brings the mind into form'.[4]

This of course is a high and arduous task, but it is central to the notion of university education. It begins, like every other journey, with elementary but indispensable steps: 'I hold very strongly that the first step in intellectual training is to impress

1. LD, XV, 380-1.
2. *Idea*, 370; the edition of the *Idea* which will be used throughout is Ian Ker's which was published with an introduction and notes at Oxford in 1976.
3. LD, XV, 380-1.
4. Ibid., 12.

upon a boy's mind the idea of science, method, order, principle, and system; of rule and exception, of richness and harmony.'[5] The pre-university phase of education needs this emphasis. The university course of studies should carry forward this preparation to a level of refined achievement. 'More intelligent members of society' should be the real outcome of university education, men and women possessing authentic 'cultivation of mind' and 'formation of the intellect'. It would follow that the man who would identify the world with one particular scientific view is not 'a teacher of liberal knowledge, but a narrow-minded bigot'.[6]

The beneficiary of a liberal education will have the life-long benefit of a 'philosophical habit of mind', a habit which is its own end and when we acquire it 'we are satisfying a direct need of our nature'.[7] In what does this habit of mind essentially consist? It is the 'power of viewing many things at once as one whole, of referring them severally to their true place in the universal system'.[8] He will naturally have studied in depth his own particular field and will enjoy the learning gleaned from those particular studies. But he will be much more than learned in one area, something that for Newman seems as dangerous as being an expert in only one book.

The second strand in Newman's notion of liberal education has to do with the university curriculum and, in particular, with the rationale of the subjects proposed and taught on the campus. Since a university 'is a place of teaching universal knowledge',[9] the unity of the many sciences, fields and disciplines should gradually create in the students a vivid sense of the richness and, in particular, of the *unity* of all knowledge. This, it seems, is the principal component in the university. And all this is clearly perceptible to reason and is validated by logic the moment one

---

5. Ibid., 12.
6. Ibid., 63.
7. Ibid., 122-3.
8. Ibid., ix.
9. Ibid., 57.

accepts the principle which Newman lays down that a university 'is a place of teaching universal knowledge'.

This justifies the inclusion of religion and theology in the curriculum of university studies. Discourse 11 makes this claim explicit. Newman saw around him the phenomenon of so-called universities both in England and in Ireland which did not offer theology in their curricula. 'An intellectual absurdity' is how he assessed this omission. 'My reason for saying so', he explains, 'runs, with whatever abruptness, into the form of a syllogism: A university, I should lay down, by its very name professes to teach universal knowledge: theology is surely a branch of knowledge: how then is it possible for it to profess all branches of knowledge, and yet to exclude from the subjects of its teaching one which, to say the least, is as important and as large as any of them?'[10] The consequences of such a gross omission, however, were particularly strident and damaging of the whole enterprise of a university education.

He emphasises two such consequences in the early Discourses. The first concerned the deformation of the whole circle of knowledge through the omission of a part. 'There is but one thought greater than that of the universe, and that is the thought of its Maker.'[11] May a seat of universal learning leave out so momentous a component of reality, such a source of truth, and still claim to be a university? He asks, not without considerable irony, 'is it wonderful that Catholics, even in the view of reason, putting aside faith or religious duty, should be dissatisfied with existing institutions, which profess to be universities, and refuse to teach theology; and that they should in consequence desire to possess seats of learning, which are, not only more Christian, but more philosophical in their construction?'[12] His appeal is to reason and not faith, and to that philosophical habit or temper of mind that justifies the inclusion of all areas of human knowl-

---

10. Dominic A. Aquila, 'A Rationale and Vision for the Natural Sciences at Franciscan University of Steubenville', in *Fellowship of Catholic Scholars Newsletter*, 2 (1996), 33.
11. Idea, 372.
12. Ibid., 84.

edge in the university curriculum and prohibits the exclusion of any 'if they come in the name of truth'.

The second consequence is equally serious. The omission of theology not only deforms the architecture of the university curriculum, it also invites the invasion of the area which theology should have occupied. 'If you drop any science out of the circle of knowledge, you cannot keep its place vacant for it; that science is forgotten; the other sciences close up, or, in other words, they exceed their proper bounds, and intrude where they have no right.'[13] Ignorance of the highest echelon of reality, the consequent deformation of the total circle of knowledge, and the inevitable invasion of the field vacated by theology, are the three most devastating results of failing to teach theology or religion.

The Unity of Truth and the Importance of Limits

It is important to recognise that a university welcomes, at least in principle, all sciences if they come in the name of truth. 'It welcomes the plurality of truths offered by each legitimate academic discipline, but it does not back away from the difficult work of ordering these truths, and securing the natural limits of each discipline.'[14] Newman particularly highlights the need for limits in order to avoid serious and damaging distortion of the 'circle' of knowledge and the tendency, so easy to understand, to make excessive demands for one's own area of knowledge. To employ an illustration used by Newman himself, the Roman Empire brought together under one ruler a hundred discordant peoples, allowed each of them its religious and cultural expressions, and vigorously resisted the aggression of particular provinces towards neighbouring provinces.[15] The fruitful partnership of the sciences and religion or theology, to take a vivid example to which we shall have to return presently, requires this respect for limits. It is no exaggeration to say that the con-

---

13. Ibid., 73-74.
14. Ibid., 375.
15. Ibid., 370-371.

flict between the two always resulted from the one invading the proper territory of the other.

The Legitimation of Theology: Surprising Significance

It is important to notice that the reasons advanced by Newman for the legitimation of religion or theology on the curriculum of a university are intellectual in character, and not religious or moral. In Newman's day many justified the inclusion of theology on religious or moral grounds. Some of these went further and saw education largely in terms of its immediately religious function. John Henry Newman emphasises the culture of the mind. He pointed to the wholeness of reality in such a way that he could brand, 'as an intellectual absurdity', the deliberate omission of religion from an institution professing to teach universal knowledge. Since a university 'brings the many disciplines into one' and aspires towards the Catholic principle of fullness, it is imperative for it not to omit the study of the highest things. Besides, this fullness is of a qualitative kind, and not of a quantitative kind.

Now all this needs to be seen in the cultural and religious context of Newman's own time. Newman read his age as an age of liberalism in religion. In what did religious liberalism consist? He defines it in a passage of impressive theoretic penetration: 'Now by liberalism I mean false liberty of thought, or the exercise of thought upon matters, in which, from the constitution of the human mind, thought cannot be brought to any successful issue, and therefore is out of place. Among such matters are first principles of whatever kind; and of these the most sacred and momentous are especially to be reckoned the truths of revelation. Liberalism then is the mistake of subjecting to human judgement those revealed doctrines which are in their nature beyond and independent of it, and of claiming to determine on intrinsic grounds the truth and value of propositions which rest for their reception simply on the external authority of the Divine Word'[16]. By the time he came to compose the discourses and lec-

16. *Apologia pro vita sua*, London and New York 1890, 288.

tures that now comprise *The Idea of a University*, he had had the time to see the dreadful havoc wrought by this assault on religious faith.

He picks up the matter in the lecture entitled, *A Form of Infidelity of the Day*. As might be expected, the form of religious liberalism considered here rejects outrightly the very thought of admitting theology into the halls of Academe since the world of religion is a world without content and substance. 'No theological doctrine is anything more than an opinion which happens to be held by bodies of men'[17] since 'nothing can be known for certain about the unseen world'.[18] 'The world of knowledge has no room for theology since theology does not give true knowledge but only opinions or theories or arguments or probabilities.'[19] In that way religion failed to meet the indispensable prerequisite for inclusion in the university curriculum, namely, that it is an area of knowledge and truth.

For Newman this agnosticism is pretentious, even preposterous. The existence of God is something that falls within the range of the intellect's activity, and most potent of all, within the purview of conscience by which we know ourselves to be addressed at the core of our being by an infinite and personal Being. As for divine revelation, it is the exhibition of new worlds of truth and reality inaccessible to unaided reason but unlimited in size and content. These worlds expand the minds of men and women. They are richly deserving of inclusion in the university curriculum.

It is true that 'not only are theology and science completely different ways of looking at the world, but they employ diametrically opposed methods, theology being deductive and science inductive'.[20] These methods, however, are the only ones appropriate in the main to the character and nature of the subject-matters which they address. In 'Christianity and Physical Science'

17. Ibid., 294.
18. *Idea*, 319.
19. Ibid., 314.
20. I. Ker, Introduction to *The Idea*, lxix.

Newman protests against the attempt to turn theology into an experimental science with 'Scripture, Antiquity, Nature ... as a foundation, on which the inductive method may be exercised for the investigation and ascertainment of that theological truth, which to a Catholic is a matter of teaching, transmission, and deduction.'[21]

Perhaps it is the final lecture on the theme of 'Christianity and Medical Science' that clinches the issue for good by showing how the abolition of one science invites the invasion of its area by another science. Thus the abolition of ethics invites medicine to forget that 'bodily health is not the only end of man, and that medical science is not the highest science of which he is the subject'. The real defect here is the failure of the medical student to realise that there are other sciences, in this case ethics, which are higher than his own and deal with vital questions and issues inevitably arising in his field. These questions are beyond the competence of his field to determine. And since truth cannot contradict truth, the medical student should have recourse to the subject of ethics for the study of the specifically moral dimensions of medicine.

Intellectual Culture still not enough

The intellectual legitimation of religion and theology in the curriculum has this radical and apologetical significance. This, however, only brings us closer to the real paradox of Newman's position. His 'eulogy of a liberal education is as it were systematically qualified by reminders of its limitations ... Newman is keenly aware of exaggerating the importance of the university and of liberal education.'[22] He stresses the absolute value of intellectual culture, it is true. There is, however, a still higher value or good, namely that of virtue and faith and religion. This fact requires some important distinctions to be put in place.

Firstly, intellectual prowess and culture is not the same as virtue or real religion which consists in obedience to Christ and

21. *Idea*, 360.
22. I. Ker, Introduction to the *Idea*, xlviii.

his word and commandments. The point is made rather dramatically in what is perhaps the best-known passage in the whole of the *Idea*, the famous 'definition of a gentleman'. The gentleman is the ideal product of a liberal education but his characteristics have nothing specifically Christian about them. Newman explains his position in these terms, '(a liberal education) makes not the Christian, not the Catholic, but the gentleman. It is well to be a gentleman, it is well to have a cultivated intellect, a delicate taste, a candid, equitable, dispassionate mind, a noble and courteous bearing in the conduct of life – these are the connatural qualities of a large knowledge; they are the objects of a university; I am advocating, I shall illustrate and insist upon them; but still, I repeat, they are no guarantee for sanctity or even for conscientiousness, they may attach to the man of the world, to the profligate, to the heartless.'[23]

Secondly, this explains a common and, as we shall see at once, accurate perception of the distinction between knowledge and religion. Newman provides a striking instance taken from the annals of church history: 'Basil and Julian were fellow-students at the schools of Athens; and one became the Saint and Doctor of the Church, the other her scoffing and relentless foe.'[24] The product of a liberal education on its own will have only 'the shallowness of philosophical religion' and not the true and authentic features of the Christian.

Thirdly, since the justification of theology in university education flows from the imperatives and nature of education itself, and so not directly from religion or Christianity, a 'higher viewpoint' is necessary for us to arrive at Newman's final position and standpoint. He has vigorously and powerfully seen off the reduction of education to the merely utilitarian level of training, and he has defended with equal vigour the independence of the university from what Ker calls 'the narrow dogmatism of a defensive clerical Catholicism'.[25] He outlines this 'higher view-

---

23. *Idea*, 110.
24. Ibid., 180-1.
25. Ker, *John Henry Newman*, Oxford 1990, 383.

point' in the IX Discourse which bears the title, 'Duties of the Church towards Knowledge'.

It is a fact that 'liberal knowledge' tends to enter 'the place of revelation'. In doing so of course it acts in a most illiberal fashion which is in flagrant contradiction of the duty to respect the integrity of other sciences and disciplines, and the concomitant duty to respect the boundaries of one's own. But that this is likely to occur in the concrete circumstances in which we find ourselves in the world, especially when under the ever-present but subtly active lash of 'those giants, the pride and passion of man', requires an equally present corrective that is strong enough to resist this tendency. What is his solution to this difficulty?

It is a most practical measure that he proposes and justifies. He proposes 'a direct and active jurisdiction of the church over (the university) and in it ... lest it should become the rival of the church within the community at large in those theological matters which to the church are exclusively committed, – acting as the representative of the intellect, as the church is the representative of the religious principle.'[26] The church as the 'representative of the religious principle' in history and humankind, and the university as 'the representative of the intellect', are liable to clash. In theory or principle this ought not to occur: truth may not conflict with truth, yes indeed, but in practice what history shows abundantly is also true, namely, they may often *seem* to contradict one another.

Now the remarkable thing about the church and the university is that this tension is altogether to be expected and is productive ultimately of good fruits. In fact, it is only the church that can provide the adequate arena for this encounter and friction of intellect and authority, of reason and revelation, of the search for truth and the claims of divinely revealed truth. Newman gives a masterly statement of this principle in Part VII of the *Apologia*: '.... it is the vast Catholic body itself, and it only, which affords an arena for both combatants (the infallible authority of the church and private judgement or reason) in that

26. *Idea*, 184.

awful, never-ending duel ... Catholic Christendom is no simple exhibition of religious absolutism, but it presents a continuous picture of authority and private judgement alternately advancing and retreating as the ebb and flow of the tide.'[27] The cut and thrust of these great protagonists, far from debilitating the energy of mind and the élan of research, only serves to heighten and to promote the development of thought, science and theology.

WHITHER UNIVERSITY EDUCATION? THE GUIDING IMPERATIVES

A. *The Unity-in-Distinction of the Many Sciences*
Newman's conception of the curriculum of university studies is based on the principle that the many constitute, both noetically and ontologically, one whole, and that it is the central function of a university 'to draw many things into one'. This architectonic principle is incomparably formulated, interestingly, in the lecture on Christianity and Scientific Investigation: 'In truth, (a university) professes to assign to each study, which it receives, its own proper place and its just boundaries; to define the rights, to establish the mutual relations, and to effect the intercommunion of one and all; to keep in check the ambitious and encroaching; ... to keep the peace between them all, and to convert their mutual differences and contrarities into the common good ... to give full play to thought and erudition in their most original forms, and their most intense expressions, and in their most ample circuit.'[28] The independence and the interdependence of the constitutive areas of knowledge is thus spelled out, together with their interaction and fruitful capacity for effective dialogue and cross-fertilisation. All this is possible and necessary since the principles of unity and dialogue have been affirmed and highlighted.

B. *The Unity-in-Distinction of Theology and the Sciences*
Historically speaking, faith and science have been in the wars for many centuries. Even the improvements in the last century

---

27. *Apo.*, 286.
28. *Idea*, 369.

are not of the magnitude to belie this statement. In Newman's vision of university education, however, there is a principled harmony between revelation and modern sciences, whether human or natural. He himself roots this harmony in the truth that both religion and science are in the final analysis the gifts of one and the same Creator. He who intends his creatures 'to sub-due the earth' (Genesis 1:28) has inspired the discovery of natur-al science by which the riches and treasures of Creation are in-creasingly yielded up for humankind's benefit. It is truth that is the pillar supporting the bridge connecting faith and the sci-ences.

As we have seen earlier, Newman also distinguishes the two kinds of knowledge in terms of different methods and goals. This distinction is crucial. Failure to recognise it lay at the root of many of the misunderstandings and conflicts between religion and science in recent centuries.

The distinction between faith and reason, however, had been carefully worked out in the thirteenth century by St Thomas Aquinas and is put forward in the First Vatican Council's teach-ing and in that of all the popes since. The church rejects the false opposition of faith and science or reason. Speaking to a confer-ence of scientists and theologians in 1991 Pope John Paul II stressed that the church could not accept the rift that developed between science and religion in the seventeenth century, 'con-vinced as she was that the truth of nature and the truth of revela-tion come from the same divine source'.[29]

It is true that in the Middle Ages theology was known as the *Regina Scientiarum*. This was the case without prejudice to the central role then occupied by the seven liberal arts, as well as by the prestigious sciences of law and medicine, in the early great medieval universities. Newman, who saw in that arrangement the happy relating and ordering of the many sciences, always stressed the hierarchy of the components of reality. If there is

29. Pope John Paul II, 'The Collaboration of Science and Religion', in *Origins*, 10 October 1991, 283; see also Pastoral Constitution on the Church in the Modern World, *Gaudium et spes*, 36; Pope John Paul II, Encyclical *Fides et Ratio* (1990).

only one idea greater than the idea of the universe, and that is the idea of the Creator of the universe, and if both philosophy and the sciences all seek an understanding of the universe (albeit from different angles), then the study of the Creator in natural theology and the Redeemer and Sanctifier of man in Catholic theology must enjoy the first place in the university. In that way a university is 'ministrative to the Catholic Church, first, because truth of any kind can but minister to truth; and next, still more, because nature ever will pay homage to grace, and reason cannot but illustrate and defend revelation.'[30]

The Pope, for his part, is the warm friend and supporter of the sciences, humanities and technology. 'He rejoices in the widest and the more philosophical systems of intellectual education, from an intimate conviction that truth is the real ally, as it is his profession; and that knowledge and reason are sure ministers to faith.'[31] The ultimate foundation, however, for this perception by Peter of the university enterprise is to be found in his conviction that all truth, whether revealed or natural, comes from the one God of nature and revelation. The God who speaks in nature cannot contradict himself when he speaks again in revelation. Newman's discussion of the Galileo case is quite interesting in this regard,[32] albeit beyond the scope of this chapter. Now all this means that, in the final analysis, Newman's conception of the university has ultimately a religious and Catholic foundation.

C. The Reconnection of Faith and Culture

All the modern popes have stressed the phenomenon of the separation of faith and culture as among the most serious, dramatic and damaging affecting our times. This separation has given birth to a world that leaves God off the agenda, as it were, in its central concerns. Faith and faith-life are thus marginalised or treated as a matter of private interest without any public signifi-

---

30. *Idea*, 370.
31. Ibid., 6.
32. Ibid., 188, 317.

cance. Religion and the church become a kind of private corporation. The result is a secular humanist experiment which tries to deal with life in all its facets as if God did not exist. *Gaudium et Spes* of the Second Vatican Council identified the issue as one of great urgency.[33]

This humanist experiment, however, has shown itself by its results. 'Technology pursued apart from the ultimate ends of human existence has demonstrated its dehumanising effect, and the shallowness of cultural estheticism has proved its inability to restore the life of the spirit in man. Reality itself has compelled a rethinking of our intellectual and educational assumptions.'[34] This rethinking of the roots of our culture is an imperative of the university that would aim at an authentic education.

This imperative opens up fascinating vistas as to the collaboration and dialogue between theology and the many sciences. 'The truth is that it is only in the mystery of the Word made flesh that the mystery of man takes on light.'[35] Jesus Christ who is the God-Man, the fullness of divinity and the fullness of humanity, has brought to history and humanity a new culture 'that introduces God to humankind, and humankind to God'.[36] He has taught us that 'it is only in the sincere gift of self that a person can find himself'.[37] He has brought to earth the culture of love as the soul of civilisation. Newman saw in the nineteenth century both the rise and the progress of that liberalism and secularism which were going to bring down 'that goodly framework of society which is the creation of Christianity.'[38]

The appropriate expansion of the human, social and economic disciplines absolutely presupposes the clear and radiant vision

33. *GS*, 53-62.
34. D. Walsh, 'The Challenge of Newman's Vision of the University', a Paper (unpublished) delivered at the International Newman Conference in Dublin, 1975, 2.
35. *GS*, 22.
36. St Irenaeus, *Against the Heresies*, III, 18, 7.
37. *GS*, 24.
38. Quoted in Christopher Dawson, *The Spirit of the Oxford Movement and Newman's Place in History, with an Introduction by Peter Nockles and a Biographical Note by Christina Scott,* London 2001, 150.

of the dignity of human beings as 'You's' before God in whose image and likeness they are made. These sciences must be in the measure of man: very emphatically, they are made for human beings, not human beings for them. This would provide at once the perfect antidote for that moral relativism that threatens the dignity of the human person. It would counteract that seeming progress of the sciences that threatens the 'abolition of man'(C. S. Lewis) by turning him into the object of sciences, and not their subject and beneficiary. A Catholic university, then, has this vital function, in the cultural and philosophical circumstances that dominate our cultural milieu, of reversing 'the most pernicious result of technological progress – more dehumanising than any actual manipulation or technique, present or future'. It will positively resist what 'we are witnessing, (namely) the erosion, perhaps the final erosion, of the idea of man as something splendid or divine.'[39]

D. The Reconnection of Thinking and Living, of Truth and Love
In *The Idea* Newman stresses the goal of third-level education as that of producing students who are 'oracles of wisdom and shrines of devotion': an education, in other words, should help students to learn not only a science or discipline, but also the difficult art of living. In other words, the purpose of existence, the true sense of our lives as intrinsically orientated to the transcendent Ground of all reality, as well as the bearing of our actions and lifestyle upon this goal, should be considered. 'Newman,' writes a famous contemporary scholar, 'manages to develop in both his personality and teaching an immediate and spontaneous union between fidelity to God and intellectual integrity without these being in conflict'.[40] It is this bonding of intellect and will, of intellectual formation and moral living at the core of the human mystery where intellect and will combine, that is a highlight of Newman's educational theory.

---

39. David Walsh, *After Ideology*, San Francisco 1990, 14.
40. L. Bouyer, 'The Permanent Relevance of Newman', in *Newman Today*, 1, San Francisco 1988, 165.

The final justification of this bonding is to be located in the specific anthropology of Newman. This consists in his understanding of conscience as the summit of the person where, in the imperative dimension of this faculty, the human being knows himself/herself to be addressed by God. Obedience to this voice is, as a result, the key to authentic human flourishing. But this voice is but a higher echelon of human consciousness which manifests itself also as the search and hunger for knowledge and truth. A truly integral education will advance along the double track of intellectual and spiritual development. A genuinely educated person, in other words, will have a love for truth and a love for goodness. He will be a person with an intellectual life and with a spiritual life. He has not only a proficiency in a science or a discipline, but also and more importantly, he has learned the art of living. In one of the sermons preached before the Catholic University of Ireland he put it like this: 'I want the same roof to contain both the intellectual and moral discipline. Devotion is not a sort of finish given to the sciences; nor is science a sort of feather in the cap, if I am so to express myself, an ornament and set-off to devotion. I want the intellectual layman to be religious, and the devout ecclesiastic to be intellectual.'[41]

To be educated is, in a word, to be prepared for the great test of life. Perhaps G. K. Chesterton puts it best of all: 'Sincerely speaking, there are no uneducated men. They may escape the trivial examinations, but not the tremendous examination of existence. The dependency of infancy, the enjoyment of animals, the love of woman, and the fear of death – these are more frightful and more fixed than all conceivable forms of cultivation of the mind. It is idle to complain of schools or colleges being trivial. Schools and colleges must always be trivial. In no case will a college ever teach the important things. For before a man is twenty, he has always learned the important things. He has learned them right or wrong, and he has learned them all alone.'[42] Allowing for Chesterton's mastery of paradox, it is easy

41. *Sermons Preached on Various Occasions*, London 1881, 13.
42. G. K. Chesterton, *A Chesterton Anthology*, San Francisco 1985, 344.

to see that an education worthy of the name must prepare people 'for the tremendous examination of existence', and it must 'teach the important things'.

E. The Rediscovery of Mind: The Overcoming of Scientism

It is well within the mark to claim that Newman spent most of his long life resisting the limitation of life, particularly its reduction to a mere this-worldly journey. His strategy was to struggle for the fullness of things in order to identify, name and challenge every narrowing down of the mystery of our existence, however subtle or sophisticated. Perhaps his *Grammar of Assent* should be read as a final creative formulation of the issue, the place where he definitively unmasked the high-sounding platitudes of rationalists and their cohorts. The wondrous growth of the natural sciences was accompanied by an implicit philosophy of knowledge according to which only the method adopted by these new sciences gave real knowledge. It had to follow that all other areas of knowledge were no longer valid. What could not be demonstrated and expressed in the language of *proof* simply did not exist. 'Thus the question of God was often scrutinised by such a method as to make it seem devoid of meaning.'[43] The worlds of ethics, of natural theology and of revelation were declared to be inexistent. And the pursuit of them was a waste of time.

Newman for his part stretches the power and the range of the mind. The mind is more versatile than any of its works, he claims, of which the natural sciences are one. It is preposterous to reduce the mind to one of its particular works. The mind can also know the existence of God and his attributes, and the great truths of the natural law. Thus Newman anticipates and responds to what has been called 'scientism', an ideology whose adherents claim that only the scientific method can yield valid knowledge. Let the scientific method work where it can, but the other fields of knowledge, such as ethics, natural theology and

43. Pope John Paul II, 'The Collaboration of Science and Religion', ibid., 283.

revelation, require methods determined by their specific sub-ject-matters, methods that are also the expressions of the human mind and therefore equally valid and reputable, intellectually speaking. In the *Grammar of Assent* Newman formulates a unit-ing epistemology that both links and differentiates the many sci-ences. His is a veritable rediscovery of mind after its mauling in the hands of scientists, rationalists and empiricists. Here he has laid philosophical foundations for an authentic 'culture of mind'.

F. True Freedom, including Academic Freedom

Closely connected with the rediscovery of mind by Newman is the idea of authentic freedom. This concept is central to Christianity and to the Catholic tradition. 'If you abide in my word, you shall be my disciples indeed, and you shall know the truth, and the truth shall make you free' (Jn 8: 31-2). Christ him-self is the fullness of truth. Accordingly, he called himself 'the truth' (Jn 14: 6). 'Christ is the guarantee that creation is orderly, coherent, and knowable. No other religion or ideology so confid-ently avers the knowability of creation which was indispensable to the rise of modern science.'[44] It follows that all the sciences, engaged as they are in the pursuit of the truth in their respective fields and according to their appropriate methods, find their ul-timate focus and fulcrum in Christ. In this perspective it is mis-taken in the extreme to suppose that the academic freedom of the sciences simply requires their emancipation from theology and from the church on the university campus.

That there might be an *apparent* clash between religion and one of the sciences is inevitable. But this is precisely one of the qualities of a truly educated mind. Such a mind is trained to be patient with such appearances and to avoid the hastiness of pro-nouncing them to be more formidable than they are in fact.

Clearly, freedom cannot be freedom *from* truth but rather freedom *to seek* the truth wherever it is to be found and accord-

---

44. Dominic A. Aquila, 'A Rationale and Vision for the Natural Sciences at Steubenville University', in *Fellowship of Catholic Scholars Newsletter*, 2 (1996), 32.

ing to the criteria and methods of one's science, without transgressing the boundaries of other sciences. It is the truth that sets free. In the Catholic vision of reality, at the centre of which are the mysteries of the incarnation and the resurrection conferring the deepest significance on the whole of creation, the love of the truth and its careful exhibition create an ethos of freedom in truth, both natural and supernatural. In such an arena it is quite unscientific to propound systematically opinions without checking their truthfulness, for this means carelessness about truth and, indirectly, the readiness to live in untruth. *Plato amicus, Aristoteles amicus, sed magis amicus veritas.*

This brings us face-to-face with a major function of the university and university education. The beneficiary of a genuine education today needs to develop a critical disposition towards the many ideas, behaviour patterns and shibboleths that circulate in contemporary society. The central questions are, *Is this true?* and *Is this good?* But it is precisely these very questions that are being marginalised in our society. Society, it is assumed, can be built on factors other than the true and the good, and men and women can find happiness independently of the true and the good. This represents a most serious corruption of mind and of the spirit. A university has the function in part of diagnosing this cancer affecting its entrails and of enabling young men and women coming through the university to inject intellectual order and spiritual order into the chaos of society. In particular, society must regain its consensus about the primacy of the things of the spirit. It must rediscover, in the words of Eric Voegelin, that 'the quest for the ground ... is the constant in all civilisations ...' The quest for the ground has been formulated in two principal questions of metaphysics. The first question is, 'Why is there something? why not nothing?' and the second is, 'Why is that something as it is, and not different?'[45] Graduates who are truly educated are properly oriented towards reality and will be the match for the false ideas that abound as to the

45. Erie Voegelin, *Conversations with Eric Voegelin*, Montreal 1980, 2.

purpose of life, the significance of our deeds, and the bearing of the latter on our final destiny.

G. A Collective Ethos of Holiness

In one of his discourses to the University of Oxford, now known as *The Oxford University Sermons*, Newman makes much of the 'collective holiness of the primitive church': 'In spite of the corruptions which disfigured it from the first, still in its collective holiness (it) may be considered to make as near an approach to the pattern of Christ as fallen man ever will attain.'[46]

For Newman Christianity is a powerfully communitarian or collective reality, since it is the reality of the life of the blessed Trinity communicated to earth in order to be the pattern and source and inspiration of the daily living of Christians. And as on the intellectual level the function of a university is 'to bring the many sciences into one', so on the higher spiritual level the function of the university is to gather its many students into unity in the sweet bonds of mutual charity (see Acts 2:42; 4:32). A university with a collective ethos invites its graduates into the adventure of going to God together since it has pleased God to save us not as individuals, but as a single people.[47]

Such a university will invite its students to live by the light they discover, to translate faith into daily attitudes, and to be responsible for each other. In that way it will highlight the importance of the other student, not as a competitor or rival, but as 'the brother for whom Christ died'(1 Cor 8:11). And if, as T. S. Eliot once wrote, devotion to one's country begins with dedication to the job in hand, then this disposition inculcated and lived throughout the days of university, is sure to produce men and women who will bring a specifically Christian contribution to society. Here indeed is the perfect antidote to that individualism that has been gaining ground in our society and which consists in an unwholesome focus on the individual and a forgetting of his duties to be his brother's keeper.

46. *Oxford University Sermons*, London 1900, 82.
47. See *Lumen Gentium*, 9.

The graduates of such an academy of learning will contribute to their particular professional, technical or academic engagements. They will possess the gifts and the principles which society needs to be both human and Christian. They are equipped to raise the tone of public life, to draw out its soul as it were. In mediaeval times the great monastic schools of Clonmacnoise and Glendalough created the soul of Irish society: perhaps a university education inspired by the vision of John Henry Newman's *Idea of a University* could go a long way towards the re-creation of this soul.

CHAPTER THREE

Understanding Faith

Any consideration of the intellectual dimension of priestly formation has to recognise the character of our times. However, these times cannot be appreciated in isolation, for they are linked to the whole history of the Western world and so can only be understood in relation to that history. Since this is the case, we shall begin by presenting a rapid cultural overview of Europe from a theological perspective. Then we shall describe the primary task of philosophical, cultural and theological education as an immersion in the Great Tradition. Next, the divine originality and newness of the Christian mystery will be highlighted: only those who have been on Mount Tabor and have caught a glimpse of 'the Lord of glory' (1 Cor 2:8) will be able to live by and communicate to their contemporaries the knowledge of Jesus Christ in which consists eternal life (Jn 17:3). Realisation is the very life of religion. Fourth, since these treasures of the gospel have to be communicated in our time which is included in God's 'mercy from age to age' (Lk 1:50), they must be coined in categories that both bring out this newness and dialogically engage the attitudes, presuppositions and insights of our scientific and technological culture with its impressive advances and equally surprising closures. This fact demands that significant readjustments be made in the style of the intellectual formation of priests before and after ordination. Finally, some key aspects of such formation will be briefly discussed.

There seem to be four great epochs in the cultural and theological history of the West. It is preferable to speak of epochs rather than eras since the former enjoy a newness that is ushered in by a spiritual event.

I. The pre-Christian epoch. This consists principally in the phenomenon of Greece and Rome.[1] Greece is synonymous with the emergence of philosophy and the breakthrough to a non mythical understanding of the divine, humanity, history and the world. By 'an effort of an almost miraculous kind', Plato and Aristotle saw that God was one and that the human being was made as a conscious longing for communion with this 'Ultimate Good' (Plato) and 'Unmoved Mover' (Aristotle). The Greeks are the discoverers of mind (*nous*) as the specifically human dimension of humankind which they define as the tension towards the Ground of Being. The truth of philosophy is personified uniquely in the dramatic events of the life of Socrates which Plato tells in three of his dialogues. Rome for its part becomes the embodiment of the practical organisational principle. Borrowing the Greek appropriation of reason, it works out the notion and practice of law (*lex*) with which it directs the daily life and political structuring of its expanding Empire.

II. The Christian epoch. 'In the fullness of time God sent his son born of woman' (Gal 4:4) and in that way the bimillennial experience of Israel was lifted on to a new plane where the synagogue becomes the church. The Christian faith spread rapidly in the whole Mediterranean basin. By the year 124 AD the learned anonymous author of the *Letter of Diognetus* could write that 'what the soul is to the body, Christians are to the Empire'.[2] This inculturation moved on two fronts, the one Greek, the other Latin. The evangelisation of the Hellenistic and Roman worlds

---

1. See P. Coda, 'La vicenda della cultura europea', in *Nuova Umanità*, 73 (1991), 19-80; Eric Voegelin, *Order and History*, III, Plato and Aristotle, Baton Rouge 1957, passim.
2. Letter to Diognetus, 6, in *Early Christian Writings*, London 1968, 177-8.

saw a unique synthesis between the gospel and culture. A learned Roman like Justin Martyr (+165 AD) captures the excitement of this first evangelisation and inculturation when he sees the gospel as the final philosophy for life.

III. The period of modernity and post-modernity. The great synthesis built up between the gospel and culture, a synthesis inspiring the daily life and cultural expression of the whole Western world, began to show strains and cracks in the late medieval centuries. Three phenomena usher in the new epoch. They were the Renaissance, the Reformation with its appalling dogmatic wars, and the Enlightenment with its *epanouissement* at the time of the French revolution. The modern world is the offspring of this movement: a mechanistic God replaces the God of Jesus Christ; morality is no longer based on revelation and the great pagan thinkers but rather on the prescriptions of closed reason; man is no longer the image and likeness of God (Gen 1:26) but the emancipated being plotting his own course; while the imperatives of liberty, equality and fraternity are disconnected from their matrix in the gospel and begin to replace the imperatives of faith, hope and charity. A world increasingly forgetful of the reality and presence of God is born. Preaching on the occasion of the opening of St Bernard's Seminary in Birmingham in 1873, Cardinal Newman described the epoch as posing an unprecedented difficulty for revealed religion: 'Christianity has never yet had experience of a world simply irreligious.'[3]

IV The contemporary search for the authentic roots. The tragic loss of contact with God in this promethean culture has motivated in many quarters a fresh hunger for God. This was particularly true of areas like Eastern Europe which until recently were subject to assaults of ideological atheism operating through totalitarian political structures. It is enough to think of a writer like Alexander Solzhenitsyn to realise the reality of this religious hunger. The new search, however, cannot lead to the mere refinding of what was lost. The searchers are now different and so

3. John Henry Newman, *Catholic Sermons*, London 1957, 123.

they will find a Christianity that will be both older and newer in its fresh vigour and revolutionary vitality for the next millennium. That revelation, it is true, 'was given to the saints once for all' (Jud 3). Still its riches are being rediscovered and appropriated afresh simply because the searchers are coming with new questions that will prepare the way for new answers.

During his visit to Spain in 1982 for the fourth centenary of the death of St Teresa of Avila, Pope John Paul II addressed the religious and cultural scenario of present-day Europeans. He was not afraid to speak of European culture as now immersed in a kind of collective 'dark night'. His words are as clear as they are incisive: 'The crises of European man are the crises of the Christian man. The crises of European culture are the crises of Christian culture. In this light, Christians can discover in the adventure of the European spirit, the temptations, infidelities and risks which belong to man in his essential relationship with God in Christ.' It is precisely this 'dark night' that purifies the mind and soul until they can 'perceive what is revealed', 'lead us to full knowledge of God', and convince us of 'the hope his call holds for us and of the rich glories he has promised his friends will inherit' (Eph 1:17-18).

PART II: IMMERSION IN THE GREAT TRADITION

The cosmological cultures of the Ancient Near East, such as those of Assyria, Mesopotamia and Egypt, experience human existence within a compact community of being. 'God and man, world and society form a primordial community of being.'[4] What stood out in these cultures was the solidarity of the four components, their compactness. This compactness took precedence over their separateness, so that the divine was experienced as omnipresent and as omnipenetrative of all the other components. Compactness, however, did not preclude the perception of an hierarchy of importance among the compact components. This perception occurs dramatically as, under the

4. Voegelin, Eric, *Order and History*, Vol 1, Baton Rouge 1956, 1.

existential impact of his all too obvious mortality, man seeks attunement to the more lasting realms, in particular, to the cosmic cycles of the planets and the biological rhythms of nature which seem to guarantee greater permanence.

As the great human drama unfolds, a clear differentiation of the four partners occurs. Historically this happens in Greece and Israel by means of philosophy and revelation, respectively. In the Old Testament record of revelation, God is the God of Abraham, Isaac and Jacob, and so the God manifested in the historical space opened up in and by the children of Abraham. Man is made in the image and likeness of God (Gen 1:26). The society of Israel is the chosen people while the world is God's good creation (Gen 1:31). With the transition to the New Testament these relationships are transformed beyond recognition. To use the language of St Irenaeus (140-210 AD), *Christus omnem novitatem attulit seipsum afferrens*[5] (Christ brought all newness by bringing himself). What happens with the event of Christ is truly staggering in as much as the ontological abyss separating the Creator and the creature is crossed: the Word who is God becomes flesh revealing the glory of the Godhead in human flesh (Jn l:14,18), so that 'here the impossible union of spheres of existence is actual' (T. S. Eliot). The People of Israel of the Old Covenant become the Body of Christ of 'the new and eternal Covenant' (1 Cor 11:25). As for God's good creation, it is resurrected with the resurrection of Christ and groans with the birthpangs of the new creation (Rom 8:19-23). The real scandal of Christianity lies in the fact that the Son of God should not only take on human nature but also the human condition in order in due course to die for the spiritually dead so that they might receive the life sent from the Father (Jn 6:57; 1:4; 10:10; 17). But more of this scandal (1 Cor 1:2) in our next section.

PART III: REALISING THE NEWNESS OF CHRISTIAN REVELATION

Although revelation is 'the initial and essential idea of Christianity' (Newman), it is not easy to realise, even a little, the

5. St Irenaeus, *Against the Heresies*, IV, 34, 1.

riches of revelation. Voltaire was closer to the mark than he may
have thought when he wrote, 'God made humankind in his
image and likeness, and humankind has paid him back.'[6] Aware
of this difficulty and feeling the steady rising pressure of religious liberalism in the early nineteenth century, John Henry
Newman feared the submerging of 'that goodly framework of
society which is the creation of Christianity'. His reaction was
not to agree with the liberals nor to throw in his lot with reac-
tionaries, but rather to have recourse to revelation as the inherent and undefeatable principle of the church's supernatural life.[7]
He aimed in all his work, as a pastor and writer, at helping people towards an imaginative and real grasp of their creed. He understood realisation 'not in an anti-intellectualistic sense, but as
the deepening of a merely notional apprehension into an existential apperception by the whole person',[8] since 'it is the whole
person who moves'.[9] We need to look now at some aspects of
revelation, for Jesus came not primarily to teach us the truth, nor
to bring us the supreme good of redemption, but above all to radiate the splendour/glory of trinitarian love in the dead heart of
history and the world.

First, Christianity announces to humans the absolute.
However, this absolute is not a monad, a block. Instead, this absolute is Trinity, and therefore complete openness and unconditional welcome. If we may use an image, the God revealed in
Jesus Christ and the Holy Spirit has a gap through which we may
enter, as the famus Rublev icon so masterfully depicts. The striking contrast between the perception of the Godhead in
Christianity, and the one God of Judaism, Islam and Plotinus
stands out. Every otherness in those latter is a simple falling away
from perfection. But in Christianity there is the fact of the other at
the very core and summit of reality: the Son is other than the
Father, and the Holy Spirit is other than the Son and the Father.

6. Bestennan, T., ed., *Voltaire's Notebooks*, Toronto 1952, 1, 231.
7. Ward, W., *Life*, 11, 415-6; 460-2.
8. Balthasar, Hans Urs von, *The Glory of the Lord*, I, Edinburgh 1982, 167.
9. John Henry Newman, *Apologia pro vita sua*, London 1890, passim.

Now while this is the simple salient truth of revelation, it is tragically true that the significance of the mystery of the Blessed Trinity has not been grasped. Both Karl Rahner and Hans Urs von Balthasar are of the opinion that if the church were to delete the Trinity from the creed, the greater part of Christian writing would be unaffected, and – what is even sadder – the lives of believers would not have to change! In other words, the core of the faith has not been appropriated at all. God-Trinity is far away from our Christian thought categories. We still have to learn to think in a Christian way and to live accordingly.

Next there is the incarnation in which 'one of the three' becomes man. He reaches us in our difference and distance from God. It is not we who reach out to him, but he reaches down to us, not clinging to his equality with God but emptying himself out to us. The utter originality of this fact needs to be noticed. '... all the other ways travelled by man to God are such as entail the overcoming of suffering, the quest for the "happy life", or immunity to the reversals of life.'[10]

Thirdly, the *kenosis* of this descent is really only the prelude to the second *kenosis* which consists in the journeying towards the cross. Here the final truths, 'the bowels of mercy of our God' (Lk 1:78), are revealed as God reigns from a tree. The crucified Son is the 'power and the wisdom of God' for 'those who are on the way to salvation' (1 Cor 1:24; 18). 'The cross alone is God's final exegesis.'[11] Alas! just as the heart is not perceived but remains hidden within the physical frame, so too the divine logic of the crucified is not realised. Here God penetrates into a realm where everything contradicts his truth, goodness, beauty and being. But it is such contradiction that he employs precisely to reveal and communicate 'the knowledge of the love that is beyond all knowing' (Eph 3:18).

The crucified Son reveals the reality of the Triune God. As recent exegetes have demonstrated, the passion narratives describe two parallel sets of handings over. Judas, one of the

---

10. Balthasar, 'God is his own Exegete', in *Communio*, 3 (1986), 284.
11. Ibid., 284.

twelve, hands Jesus over to the Jewish authorities, who in turn hand him over to the Romans, who then hand him over to death on the patibulum. However, a second set of handings over now comes into view, and it is this set that primarily interests the New Testament writers. The Father hands over his Son in the sense that he inspires him with the love by which he gives himself up for us (Rom 8:39). The Son loves us and gives himself up for us (Gal 2:20). Finally, the dying Son yields up the Spirit to us (Jn 19:30). Thus the cross is a trinitarian drama: Jesus crucified is the icon of the Blessed Trinity. He is the manifestation and concretisation of the eternal triune love that constitutes God ('God is love', 1 Jn 4:8,16). Here we arrive at a conception of God which is 'so great that none greater can ever be thought' (St Anselm).

In the very moment where the sin of the world is most highlighted, the ever greater goodness of God the Holy Trinity is both revealed and communicated. 'Where sin increased, grace abounded all the more' (Rom 5:20 RSV). This is precisely the import of the pre-Pauline phrase 'for us' which occurs in the texts quoted above. And little wonder that St John admonishes believers to 'look on the one they have pierced' (Jn 19:37).

Fourthly, because the God of Jesus Christ is Trinity and so a communion of infinite persons, the Christian gospel teaches the way to the brother as well as the way to God. As 'the brother for whom Christ died' (1 Cor 8:11), each person is a sacrament-presence of Christ, an ever present reminder of the blood that was shed for us all (1 Pt 2:18-9) and of the abandonment that was endured (Mk 15:34; Mt 27:46) by the one mediator (1 Tim 2:5). It is altogether logical, then, that the central commandment in the gospel, the one Jesus calls both 'new' and 'his' (Jn 13:34; 15:12), is 'love one another as I have loved you' (Jn 15:12). Jesus gives that commandment in order to achieve an extrapolation on earth of the life of reciprocal love at the heart of the Blessed Trinity, his homeland, 'Father, may they be one in us, as you are in me and I am in you, so that the world may believe it was you who sent me' (Jn 17:21). Just as the immigrant to a foreign country has to adapt to the customs, culture and language of another people, but also loves to bring with him the life of his homeland, so in like manner Christ, one of the Eternal Three, made himself one with humankind in the incarnation and abandonment on Golgotha, but brought into humankind and history the life of his homeland as the life of infinite mutual love among infinite persons. Here 'vistas closed to human reason open up' (*Gaudium et Spes*, 24). We must first realise that Christian living based on the New Commandment is 'the synthesis of the gospel' (John Paul II) and, more importantly, begin the adventure of living it. In this way we could discover the meaning of the 'definition' of the church given in *Lumen Gentium* as 'a people made one from the unity of the Father, the Son and the Holy Spirit' (par 4). Christians living in this manner would exert a powerful attracting force on others, just as the prototypical Pentecost community in Jerusalem did (Acts 2:47; 4:21, 33; 5:13).

What is the great task of pastors today as we face 'the challenge of the New Evangelisation to which our Lord is calling the church on the threshold of the third millennium?'[12] A recent author puts the answer in clear terms, 'It is up to Christians of our day to proclaim their faith in order that the world might rediscover God in an ontological and spiritual relation. This great responsibility might distress us, but remains for all that among the most important in the history of Christianity. God tells us to fear nothing and to proclaim his good news. It is about time Christians, and above all Christian theologians understood that what is called for is not adaptation to the world's thought, but the proclamation of the God of revelation, willingly accepting the eventual scandal. This is, in my opinion, the true evangelisation.'[13] As with the apostle Paul who was so persuaded of the scandal in the proclamation of a crucified Messiah, we must not be ashamed of the gospel, for it is God's power to save all, the faithful and the lapsed, the religious and the secularised.

12. Pope John Paul II, *Pastores Dabo Vobis*, London 1992, 51.
13. Vloet, John van der, 'Faith and the Postmodern Challenge' in *Communio*, 2 (1990), 140; see Kasper, W., 'Is God Obsolete?', in *Irish Theological Quarterly*, 2 (1989), 85-98; Second Vatican Council, The Dogmatic Constitution on Divine Revelation, *Dei Verbum*, 1.

PART IV: 'IN THE CIRCUMSTANCES OF TODAY'

We looked at the present period of our history albeit in very summary fashion, in our opening section when we tried to contextualise our subject. Whatever terminology is employed to describe this period, we may speak of our contemporary cultural scenario as one of closure against the transcendent. In our times God is frequently left off the agenda of humankind in the great fora of law and education, economics and communications, medicine and planning. This crisis is the crisis of European and Christian man, since its roots are deep in the drama of the European experience.

Joachim of Fiore, the Calabrian abbot and follower of St Francis, adopted a kind of trinitarian millenarianism: he proposed a Third Age of the Holy Spirit which could be ushered in by the appropriate human endeavour. 'My divine future is drawn within the movement of time and falls within the scope of human planning.'[14] It was a short step to the emancipation of humankind from God altogether. 'Man's mission to be creative was misunderstood as a charge to accomplish everything himself, thus approximating more nearly the fall of man than the account of creation.'[15] Humankind had outlasted God and was at least as wise (Gen 3: 5)! Such a radical anthropomorphism makes God obsolete, and boldly proclaims the new categorical imperatives of progress and pluralism, of freedom and socialism.

The secularised world, however, is running into its own self-made trouble. The crisis of God is now leading to the crisis of humankind or, if one prefers, the abolition of God is initiating the abolition of man. 'God is dead; Marx is dead, and even I do not feel too well'! Without meaning, unconditional meaning, and without God human existence is ultimately absurd. The temptation and experiment of Godless humanism as manifested

14. See the masterly analysis in Voegelin, E., *The New Science of Politics*, Chicago and London 1952.
15. Henrici, P., 'Modernity and Christianity' in *Communio*, 2 (1990), 149-150.

in the great apocalyptic movements of our times has only led to the cancellation of humankind's real dignity since human beings become the mere function of matter (materialism), time (Marxism), and the technology of biological reproduction. This nihilistic impasse of modernity may justly be interpreted as the *reductio ad absurdum* of its first principles, for the fault always lies in the roots. Perhaps Shakespeare's character Prospero in *The Tempest* puts the matter in the clearest terms:

Now I want
Spirits to enforce, art to enchant;
And my ending in despair
Unless I be relieved by prayer,
Which pierces so that it assaults
Mercy itself and frees all fault.

Now it is to such a world, a world rich in scientific and technological achievement and promising even more, that the Church must communicate its ever young and ever ancient gospel. There are, it seems, three central emphases which the magisterium of the church is highlighting in our times.[16] The first of these relates to the revision of ecclesiastical studies. Here 'the first object in view must be a better integration of philosophy and theology.'[17] The point of this integration is that 'these objects should work together harmoniously to unfold ever increasingly to the minds of seminarians the mystery of Christ.'[18] The wisdom of the Council shines out in the emphasis it places on philosophy, for the weakness of contemporary culture lies in its deformation of human reason. 'We do not live,' writes Eric Voegelin, 'in a post-Christian, or "post philosophical" or "neo-pagan" age, or in the age of a "new myth" or of "utopianism", but plainly in a period of massive deculturation through the deformation of reason.'[19] If intellect is made for truth, how serious

16. See PDV, 51-6.
17. Second Vatican Council, *Optatam Totius*, 14.
18. Ibid.
19. E. Voegelin, 'The Gospel and Culture', in *The Collected Works*, Vol 12, Baton Rouge and London 1990, 178.

must be its deformation! An authentic philosophical training will have to lead the student to the root of such deformation. In the process it ought to create in the student a love for the truth.

Philosophical studies, for example, will have the task of tracing the derailment of mind since the religious and scientific revolutions of the sixteenth century when a particular usage of human intelligence, namely, that in the new 'natural sciences', began to be put forward as not only the only valid usage of intellect but also as the very nature of the mind with the consequence that all other usages of reason were now declared either 'prescientific' or simply irrational. As a result, religion, metaphysics, ethics and aesthetics were labelled as belonging to the world of feeling and so as unfit for the university. They could not be the subject of 'science'![20] And the consequence is that the vast majority of modern universities no longer include theology. And still 'the quest for the Ground ... is a constant in all civilisations ... The quest for the ground has been formulated in two principal questions for metaphysics. The first question is, "Why is there something; why not nothing?" and the second is, "Why is that something as it is, and not different?"'[21] Having shown that 'the question of God, then, lies within man's horizon',[22] philosophy must then show 'the links between the great philosophical questions and the mysteries of salvation which are studied in theology under the higher light of faith'.[23]

The second emphasis in the area of intellectual formation is that of the particular categories to be employed in the work of evangelisation. Already we have suggested that the objective mystery of Christ demands a language both faithful to its revelation in scripture and tradition, and sensitive to the particular cultural ethos of our time. The warrant and precedent for such sensitivity are present in the history of the church. In this century

20. Newman realised the implications of this dramatic phenomenon with singular perspicacity: see *Oxford University Sermons, Idea of a University*, etc.
21. E. Voegelin, *Conversations*, 2.
22. Lonergan, Bernard, *Method in Theology*, London 1972, 103.
23. *PDV*, 52.

one might point to illustrious instances where this engaging of culture was effectively achieved. Hans Urs von Balthasar employed the personalism of Rudolf Allers and Martin Buber who see in interpersonality the objective medium of human existence. Karl Rahner blended St Thomas and Heidegger, while Karl Wojtyla utilised the categories forged by Scheler and Husserl. Is it possible to adopt the themes of liberty, progress and pluralism in order to draw out the 'new things and old' of the gospel? And would such adoption not be an instance of the dialogue which Pope Paul VI and Vatican II laid down for the church? But what a challenging theological task confronts the theological community in setting out on the way of dialogue! And the student of theology preparing for the ministry! Still this has been the time-tried method of evangelisation and inculturation throughout the history of the church. The category and the theme of liberty, for example, could be engaged in order to present the core of divine revelation as the divine liberation of humankind in the missions of Christ and of the Holy Spirit. In that way the Letter to the Galatians would take on a fresh relevance.

A third emphasis in the intellectual formation of priests is the closer linking of theology and spirituality. This is the vital corrective to a theological style which has been in the ascendancy since roughly the fourteenth century. That style underlines the intellectual scientific character of theology and philosophy to the extent that they lose contact with the Christian life. It assumed that faith-life and the science of faith could operate largely in isolation from one another. The fruit of this unhappy separation was a theological science disconnected from spirituality, and a spirituality unconnected with theology. Historically speaking, this divorce was a tragic innovation with respect to the happy marriage of Christian thinking (theology) and Christian living (spirituality) of the first millennium, in fact until and including the great scholastics of the thirteenth century. Of it Hans Urs von Balthasar writes, 'In the whole history of Catholic theology there is hardly anything that is less noticed, yet more deserving of notice, than the fact that, since the great period of scholasticism, there have been few theologians who were saints. We mean here by theologian one whose office and vocation is to expound revelation in its fullness, and therefore who centres on dogmatic theology.' This schism between theology and spirituality has been a more serious bloodletting for the church than the Great Eastern Schism and the Reformation. The result has been 'on the one hand, the bones without the flesh, "traditional theology"; on the other the flesh without the bones, that very pious literature that serves up a compound of asceticism, mysticism, spirituality and rhetoric.'[24] It is obvious that this mutually damaging separation has to be overcome in order to bring truth and life, thinking and living, *logos* and *ethos* together again.

Now this contention is not made in the abstract. One often meets people who never had the opportunity to study the faith in a formal manner and still they have a profound understanding of the faith. Such people have already encountered the God of the living and they are now capable of giving an account of their hope to anyone who asks (1 Pet 3:15). In the light of this happy phenomenon, it seems particularly tragic if those studying the faith in theology see but little connection between the following of Christ and the study of this revelation of which he 'is both mediator and fullness'.[25] In the words of *Pastores Dabo Vobis*, 'theological reflection is centred on adherence to Jesus Christ, the wisdom of God: mature reflection has to be described as a sharing in the "thinking" of Christ (cf 1 Cor 2:16) in the human form of a science.'[26]

We can take an example or two to illustrate the point. A theology of the Blessed Trinity is likely to sound very abstract and removed from life if there is little or no life of community and fraternity among the students. If there is an effort being made to live in mutual caring and interest, students will more easily perceive the life of the triune God as a transcendent communion of infinite persons who are the one God. Furthermore, this theolog-

24. Balthasar, *The Word Made Flesh*, San Francisco 1989, 193.
25. Vatican Two, *Dei Verbum*, 2.
26. *PDV*, 53.

ical perception will inspire them to live this adventure of mutual love even more thoroughly. And the fruits in the life of such a student are special, for 'the "new man" is one who passes from death to life because, as a member of Christ's body, he knows how to live for the other members of Christ's body.'[27] Or to take a second example. The tract on grace links with prayer which is the life of grace rising up to its conscious articulation in the believing, hoping and loving Christian. If grace consists especially in the indwelling of the divine persons in the heart of the justified person, then prayer ought to be practised and understood as a communion with the Father, the Son and the Holy Spirit. And what light this would throw on the abiding format of liturgical prayer wherein the community prays to the Father through the Son in the Holy Spirit!

Our considerations have come full circle. We began by studying the intellectual formation of priests at the conclusion of the second millennium. We saw that the anthropocentrism of our times demands a search for the deeper roots of our faith. Secondly, this does not mean a conforming to the times but an immersion in the Great Tradition which is life and light (Rom 12). Then we reflected on the need for a fresh realisation of the wonder and originality of the tradition, indicating in the process four striking aspects of the mystery of faith. Fourthly and finally, the communication of the gospel in 'the circumstances of our times' demands deeper integration between key areas of the priest's life. Among the areas needing this deeper unity are philosophical and theological formation, theological and spiritual formation, and faith and culture.

CHAPTER FOUR

The Education of Catholics for the Mission according to Cardinal Newman

In the month of October 1850 an announcement was made which shook the whole of England: the Catholic hierarchy was to be restored in the land. After its banishment two hundred years previously it was now being set up again. 'It is difficult to realise the fury caused. Protest meetings were held all over England, the Pope and Cardinal Wiseman were burned in effigy ... The agitation showed the strength of English Protestantism.'[1] The net effect of the agitation was that the bishops were effectively silenced. Convinced that the church was not only the hierarchy but all the People of God, Newman wrote to a friend, 'I dare say it may be in the event advisable for our bishops to do nothing – but for that reason, if for no other, the laity should stir.'[2] The hour of the laity had struck.

What kind of lay faithful?

But what kind of laity? From the time he joined the Catholic communion five years previously in 1845 he was increasingly aware of the inadequate preparation of the lay people for the mission now falling to them. In particular, they needed education and formation for the task ahead. At the end of *Lectures on the Present Position of Catholics in England,* delivered in 1850 in reply to the attack on the bishops (G. K. Chesterton described it as having been practically preached to a raging mob), he described the kind of laity he wanted for the times now upon Catholics in England. It is worth quoting this purple passage,

---

1. C. S. Dessain, *John Henry Newman,* London 1966, 99.
2. J. H. Newman, *Letters and Diaries,* XIV, London 1963, 216; all Newman works are referred to in the standard edition published by Longmans, Green, and Co, London.

'Your strength lies in your God and your conscience; therefore it lies not in your number. It lies not in your number any more than in intrigue, or combination or worldly wisdom. What I desiderate in Catholics is the gift of bringing out what their religion is. I want an intelligent, well-instructed laity; I am not denying you are such already: but I mean to be severe and, as some would say, exorbitant in my demands. I wish you to enlarge your knowledge, to cultivate your reason, to get an insight into the relation of truth to truth, ... to understand how faith and reason stand to each other, what are the bases and principles of Catholicism. In all times the laity have been the measure of the Catholic spirit; they saved the Irish church three centuries ago, and they betrayed the church in England.'[3] Here one finds some of the key themes in Newman's blueprint for the education and the formation of Catholics for the mission then as well as now.

In this chapter I should like to address the issue of Newman's message for the education of Catholics in the England of his day, and then apply the message to the education of Catholics for their mission in our times. In setting out towards that goal I will link the different dimensions of education by means of the theme of integrity. These dimensions are as follows: first, the integrity of conscience as the key to the harmony between the soul and God, as well as between religion and intellectual honesty. Second, we will look at that special integrity of everyday living which is holiness. Third, we will focus on the integrity of our understanding of the church, in particular integrity in understanding her apostolic origin and catholicity. Newman's was a most realistic appraisal of the church's history and of the particular drama of the church in the modern and enlightened era. Fourth, the Catholic Newman set about the remedying of the practical deficiencies he observed in the Catholic community of his day, a major aspect of which was the provision of better opportunities for Catholics in the field of education. This concern of Newman may be called the integrity of education. These four integrities, then, may be called the four pillars of education for the mission.

---

3. *Present Position of Catholics in England*, 388-91.

I. The Integrity of Conscience:
Moral and Religious Education

'Your strength lies in your conscience.' The fact of conscience was of first importance for Newman. 'Whether a man has heard the name of the Saviour of the world or not, he has within his breast a certain commanding dictate, not a mere sentiment, not a mere opinion, or impression, or view of things, but a law, an authoritative voice, bidding him to do certain things and avoid others. I do not say that its particular injunctions are always clear, or that they are always consistent with each other; but what I am insisting on here is this, that it commands, that it praises, it blames, it promises, it threatens, it implies a future, and it witnesses the unseen. It is more than a man's own self. The man himself has no power over it, or only with extreme difficulty; he did not make it, he cannot destroy it.'[4]

For Newman conscience has two central aspects: it is a moral sense or judgement, and it is a moral imperative. It tells us what is right and wrong, and it tells us to do what is right. Conscience is a voice with two simultaneous, but distinct, messages, the first one enabling us to know right and wrong, the second commanding us to do the right and avoid the wrong.

The second message Newman found to be fascinating, for it makes us realise that in and through conscience we are addressed. And we know ourselves to be addressed! Conscience in this mode is the voice of the Creator speaking to the core of our being, to the heart which is not emotion but the very centre of our being. This makes of conscience the connecting principle between the Creator and his creature. Conscience, then, is the key to our first relationship with our Creator.

The other dimension of conscience as moral judgement enables us to know what is right and what is wrong. It is the faculty for gaining moral truth, just as intellect is the faculty for finding the truth. As such it is the source of ethics and morality.

In order to be in touch with oneself, then, it is first necessary

---

4. *Oxford University Sermons*, 64.

to be in touch with conscience where God speaks to us. Listening to conscience one is sensitive to the things of God, as well as in touch with the duty to seek the truth and, having found it, to live by the truth. 'Newman manages to develop in both his personality and teaching an immediate and spontaneous union between fidelity to God and intellectual integrity without these being in conflict.'[5] From the time of his decisive religious experience at the age of fifteen, the voice of conscience and the imperatives of reason and of intellect are in perfect harmony.

This conviction permeates all his later work. To take but one instance, he claims that a university should produce men and women who are both prayerful and intellectual, or to use his images, 'shrines of devotion and oracles of knowledge'. In fact, the great danger of the age, as he saw it, was the separation of religion and reason, theology and the sciences. Such separation deforms the very notion of education and reduces the university to either a place of training or an ambience for the imparting of knowledge. This claim runs through *The Idea of a University* from beginning to end. Religion when it is authentic (he preferred the word 'real'), makes us both obedient to God and hungry for the truth in all areas. 'As God is unconditionally the master of our thinking as of our acting, rationality and obedience cannot be opposed, being one in their root.'[6]

Great realist that he was, John Henry Newman was well aware that, since conscience 'is a stern monitor', many will dislike their own inner teacher. More than that, he saw all around him a gathering opposition to the place and role of conscience in both individual and society. In the *Letter to the Duke of Norfolk* he writes: 'Conscience is a stern monitor, but in this century it has been superseded by a counterfeit, which the eighteen centuries prior to it never heard of, and could not have mistaken for it, if they had. It is the right of self-will.'[7] Over one hundred years

---

5. L. Bouyer, 'The Permanent Relevance of Newman', in *Newman Today*, I, San Francisco 1988, 165.
6. *Ibid*.
7. *Difficulties of Anglicans*, II, 250.

have elapsed since that diagnosis of Newman, a hundred years in which we have unfortunately seen the verification of that prediction. Newman's insight here brings to mind the comment attributed to the famous evangelist, Billy Graham: 'To follow one's conscience today is a bit like following a wheelbarrow: you generally end up where you want to go.' Conscience has become the right to do what one *wants* to do, not do what one *ought* to do, what God tells us in our inner heart, or what a wise tradition tells us or what the church tells us.

II. THE INTEGRITY THAT IS HOLINESS:
SPIRITUAL EDUCATION

'Your strength lies in your God'.

After his teenage conversion to a serious and genuine religious existence in 1816, Newman borrowed a motto from Thomas Scott, an Evangelical of the Calvinist school, whom he always regarded as the person to whom, under God, he owed his soul. That motto was, 'Holiness before Peace'. In the first of his published sermons he elaborated the theme, Holiness necessary for future Blessedness.[8] Contemporaries testify that the sermon made his hearers pensive, even anxious.

Name-dropping is generally considered to be bad form. There is a story about an Irish politician who said in company, 'There is too much name-dropping in the country, and President McAleese and I are very worried about it.' There is too much name-dropping in Newman studies too. What I mean is all those names by which the figure of Cardinal Newman is known: freedom of conscience, emphasis on the laity and their role in the church and the world, the development of doctrine, defence of the episcopacy and the infallibility of the Pope, and so on. Unfortunately, he is often reduced to this – a name and a few labels. Now this reduction to a few names and titles often leads people to exclaim, Would the real Newman please stand up? Would the real candidate for canonisation please stand up?

---

8. *Parochial and Plain Sermons*, I, 1-14.

Now what seems to stand out in Newman's journey is the sheer attractiveness and relevance of his spiritual adventure for God. Though always committed to self-denial, Newman eventually decided against the way of extreme asceticism. However, he elaborated and taught to many others a way of holiness. In his *Meditations and Devotions* he formulates this way as follows: 'He, then, is perfect who does the work of the day perfectly, and we need not go beyond this to seek perfection. You need not go out of the round of the day. I insist on this because I think it will simplify our views, and fix our exertions on a definite aim. If you ask me what you are to do in order to be perfect, I say, first: do not lie in bed beyond the time of rising; give your first thoughts to God; make a good visit to the Blessed Sacrament; say the Angelus devoutly; eat and drink to God's glory; say the Rosary well; be recollected; keep out bad thoughts; make your evening meditation well; examine yourself daily; go to bed in good time, and you are already perfect.'[9]

It would be a major misapprehension, however, to conclude that Newman thought that holiness consisted exclusively in saying one's prayers, getting up on time and going to bed punctually, in a kind of doing ordinary things extraordinarily well. There was something more about his vision. One scholar puts it in one succinct formula, 'He is the epitome of *credal-shaped holiness*.'[10]

What does credal holiness mean? Newman noticed that the very structure of the Creed was trinitarian: the Father so loved us that he gave us his only Son who is both the Father's way to us and to our human condition, as well as our way to the Father. That Son made flesh for us then sends us his and the Father's Spirit to draw us into communion with himself and so with the Father. The Creed is really a liturgical hymn to this divine and human drama. Thus for Newman Christianity is the presence of Persons, the presence of the Father, the Son and the Holy Spirit to us. We are baptised into their presence, their communion, so

9. *Meditations and Devotions*, 328-9.
10. M. Sharkey, 'Newman 's Quest for Holiness in His Search for the Truth ', in *Newman Today*, 178.

that, in the words of St Paul, we 'have in the one Spirit our way to come to the Father' (Eph 2:18). Here is the essential truth of our humanity and graced being as baptised, eucharistised and confirmed Christians. And this truth sets up the imperative of holiness: Become what you are! Holiness is the basic vocation, the very badge of the Christian who for his part must live by the supreme grace and gift of the presence of the divine Persons.

In his second novel, *Callista*, written in 1855, Newman describes a decayed Christian community in North Africa in the third century. The heroine of the story, which sets out to paint vividly the life of those early Christians, is the pagan image-maker, Callista. The priest, Caecilius (St Cyprian), explains to her about Our Lord: 'The nearer we draw to him, the more triumphantly does he enter into us; the longer he dwells in us, the more intimately have we possession of him. It is an espousal for eternity. This is why it is so easy for us to die for our faith, at which the world marvels.'

As for Callista, she turns over in her mind this and what two other Christians, a female slave and a country youth, had told her. 'Now the three witnesses who had addressed her about Christianity had each of them made it consist in the intimate divine presence in the heart. It was the friendship or mutual love of person with person. Here was the very teaching which already was so urgently demanded both by her reason and her heart, which she found nowhere else.'[11] With that vivid sense of the real and the good, he was always worried about the danger of unreality and insincerity in religion. 'It is easy to be religious on paper', he used to say. His whole life of writing, researching, teaching, and communicating always had only one goal: Live what you profess! 'I want a man on the one hand to confess his immortality with his lips, and on the other, to live as if he tried to understand his own words, and then he is in the way of salvation.'[12]

It is striking to notice how much Newman's thinking antici-

11. *Callista*, 222, 293
12. *Parochial and Plain Sermons*, I, 24.

pates the thought of the Second Vatican Council in this respect. Its Dogmatic Constitution on the Church, *Lumen Gentium*, refuses to present the mystery of the church except as a way of holiness. Chapter IV bears the title, *The Universal Call to Holiness*. Again in the Decree on Ecumenism, *Unitatis Redintegratio*, there is an equally stimulating call to, and explanation of, the imperative of holy living as the soul of Christianity and the indispensable pre-supposition of the restoration of unity among all the followers of Christ.

What would Newman say to us today in the midst of the storms that blow around us? Surely he would encourage us to live the Council, to translate the call of the Council into a pro-gramme of daily living.[13] He assured his congregations in the 1830s that they must win Christ's battles through the integrity of their lives and lifestyle: 'He who obeys God conscientiously, and lives holily, forces all about him to believe and tremble before the unseen power of Christ.'[14]

What stands out in particular relief in his teaching on the in-tegrity that is holiness is the connection between right belief and right living or, if you like, between doctrine and holiness. All the doctrines of the faith have a practical character. We are made holy by receiving, dwelling on, and entering into doctrine. Thus the central doctrines of the Creed are the very map of the holy journey of Christians: the two missions of the Son and the Holy Spirit like two great arms let down from heaven open out the life of the Blessed Trinity to us, yes, but these same missions map out the sure and certain way to the Father's house. 'I am the Way, the Truth and the Life. No one comes to the Father except through me' (Jn 14:6). And just as the doctrines of the faith teach the Way to the Father, so they also teach the way to the brother, who is always 'the brother for whom Christ died' (1 Cor 8:11).

---

13. Ian T. Ker, 'Newman and the Postconciliar Church', in *Newman Today*, 121-42.
14. *Parochial and Plain Sermons*, I, 292.

III. The Integrity of our Understanding of the Church: Change and Continuity

'I wish you to understand what are the bases and principles of Catholicism.'

One hundred and sixty-one years ago, Fr Dominic Barberi, a Passionist missionary from outside Rome and working on the English mission, received Newman into what Newman was convinced 'was the one fold of the Saviour'. That dramatic step concluded an enormous spiritual, theological and personal journey. Pope Paul VI described it 'as the most toilsome, but also the greatest, the most meaningful, the most conclusive, that human thought ever travelled during the last century, indeed one might say during the modern era'.[15] In other words, Newman lived through enormous change.

Ours is a time of profound change too. We have a natural inclination to seek the security of permanence, so that religion, the anchor and harbour of our very life here below, should always be that which was always the same, everywhere the same, and accepted as such by everyone ('*quod semper, quod ubique, quod ab omnibus:* that which was accepted always, everywhere, and by all'). And we live in a time when change seems to be the rule, and stability seems to be the exception.

Of course one expects fluidity in the world of fashion, where last year's designs are discarded and this year's will soon be passé. The world of technology is a world of the most rapid change, a world where obsolescence seems to be built into products. A computer tends to be obsolete before its operator has learned how to use it! In fact, it is hard to think of any area in modern life where change and obsolescence are not formidable, frequent and sometimes frustrating facts.

Not even the world of religion, where fidelity and perseverance and commitment are customarily considered virtues, has escaped the pervasive phenomenon of change. But how are peo-

---

15. Pope Paul VI, *L'Osservatore Romano*, 28 October 1963; *AAS*, 1963, 1025.

ple going to cope with change? There are some people who mimic the world of fashion and change their theology every year. Others abandon their efforts to keep pace with change like a frustrated computer trainee who turns off the machine and looks for another occupation. But some seek to find a balance between change and continuity, and many of these have been fortunate enough to discover a sound mentor to guide them in their religious pilgrimage: John Henry Newman.

Newman's autobiography, the *Apologia pro Vita Sua*, has the subtitle, 'a history of my religious opinions'. He describes this history as the story of definite stages. The stages are as follows: 'the conventional piety of a middle-class English family where the Bible was read but where religious enthusiasm was suspect. The evangelical fervour prompted by an adolescent conversion experience; the determined search for an ecclesial community that would afford doctrinal certainty amidst the changing course of history.' As he passed through these different stages, his 'religious opinions' gradually changed as they were incorporated into a theological vision of the church's continuity through history.[16]

The great question for Newman as he discovered the church in and with his discovery of the Fathers was, 'Has the church of the apostles and the Fathers such as St Athanasius and St Ambrose continued down to the present?' During the years of the Oxford Movement he tried to infiltrate the principles of the great Fathers into the Anglican Church of the day. At the time he subscribed to the so-called 'Branch Theory' of the church, according to which the one church of the apostles had expressed itself in the threefold of the Orthodox, the Catholic and the Anglican communions. By the early 1840s, however, his mind had shifted drastically under the impact of fresh discovery. For example, he was convinced that the Anglican Church was apostolic in as much as it had been faithful to the revelation given to the apostles and taught in the early Ecumenical Councils. The

---

16. John T. Ford, 'Faithfulness to Type in Newman's "Essay on Development"' in *Newman Today*, 17-8.

Roman Church held the same truths of teaching, liturgy and structure, but had introduced during the second millennium teachings and practices not present in revelation, teachings not given in scripture and the Fathers. These had to be corruptions of the apostolic faith given once for all to the saints (Jude 3).

But perhaps these same additions might be plausible, even credible, if it could be shown that they were possible developments, that is unfoldings of the revelation, and so not arbitrary additions. By 1844 he felt strongly enough in favour of this hypothesis to start writing about the matter. This is the immediate context and inspiration of the *Essay of the Development of Christian Doctrine*. Has the church of the apostles continued down to this day? If so, which church is that continuation? The essay 'is not so much a study in comparative dogmatics as an "identity test".'[17]

Perhaps the title of this theological classic is somewhat misleading. The intention of the book is not to give an explanation of how dogma develops. Rather, it aims at showing the essential continuity between the church of the apostles and the Fathers, and the Catholic Church of the nineteenth century. Long before he had reached the actual end of the book, he was certain of the conclusion: the church founded by Christ on the apostles still continues in history, not as a museum version of the original, but in a continuity that harmonises permanence and development. And this seemed to be a dramatic instance of the principle, 'In a higher world it is otherwise, but here below to live is to change, and to be perfect is to have changed often.'[18]

IV REMEDYING PRACTICAL DEFICIENCIES: INTEGRITY IN THE FORMAL EDUCATION OF CATHOLICS

We have already mentioned his abiding interest in education, and specifically third-level education. Now the university provides the arena, as it were, where these vital concerns can be addressed. This explains the enthusiasm with which he took up

17. *Ibid.*, 19
18. *Development of Christian Doctrine*, 40.

Cardinal Cullen's invitation to begin the foundation of the Catholic University in Dublin. Only a university could provide that 'culture of the intellect' without which Catholics would be unequipped to take their part in the world and society. University education properly received would have the effect of 'real cultivation of mind' in an 'intellect ... properly trained and formed to have a connected view or grasp of things'.[19] This goal, however, is quite unattainable without a consensus in the university milieu concerning the even more important life of the Spirit. 'At a time of emerging utilitarianism, specialisation and secularism in education he raised his voice on behalf of the classical ideal of the spiritual and intellectual development of the inner man.'[20]

With clear foresight Newman detected the march of mind of the Enlightenment, what he called religious 'liberalism'. It had developed a masterly strategy in order to keep religion and theology out of the university. In response Newman sought to counter the central contention of the Enlightenment that 'Religion is not the subject-matter of science'. This modern 'form of infidelity'[21] was based on the denial of revelation and the reduction of its contents to the status of opinion and sentiment. In *The Idea of a University* he returns to the ideal of relating knowledge and spiritual truth within the guiding objective of the university. It is no surprise, then, that this ardent advocate of 'liberal education' aimed at an inclusive goal for university education when he writes unambiguously: '... when the church founds a university, she is not cherishing talent, genius, or knowledge, for their own sake, but for the sake of her children, with a view to their spiritual welfare and their religious influence and usefulness, with the object of training them to fill their respective posts in life better, and of making them more intelligent, capable, active members of society'.[22]

---

19. *Idea*, 10-11.
20. David Walsh, 'The Challenge of Newman's Vision of the University', paper delivered at Newman Conference in Dublin, 1982, 1.
21. *Idea*, 310-27.
22. *Ibid.*, 7.

One cannot but be struck by the manner in which Newman anticipates the secular humanist experiment whose beginnings he so perceptively described. This experiment has run its course. The results are clear to all: the loss of spiritual reality, the consequent demise of ultimate purposefulness in life, a technology and science expanding without sense of the ultimate dignity of the human being and therefore devoid of ethical guidance or theological critique. This leads to a situation where the meaning of human life is out of view and there is an eerie silence about the essentials. The Belfast-born theologian, C. S. Lewis, saw in this development nothing less than 'the abolition of man'.[23]

I have suggested the theme of integrity as the guiding and linking theme in the life of John Henry Newman whom Pope John Paul II described as 'that pilgrim for truth'.[24] That integrity is written into human conscience, where each person can know himself to be addressed by God and so can grow, with the help of divine grace, in the true sense of his human dignity. This 'address' from God is, secondly, the beginning of the call to put God in the first place. Putting God in the first place sets a man or a woman on the greatest of all adventures, the adventure of holiness with the assistance of divine grace. This, in turn, leads on to the mystery of the church as the concrete embodiment, or sacrament, in history of the religious principle. Newman's educational philosophy spells out the implications of these principles in the world of learning and study.

What kind of lay faithful did Newman desire to see in the church and in the world? Men and women ready for the mission, men and women of integrity, who know that their strength lies not in their number but in their fidelity to conscience, in the integrity of a sincere response to the call to everyday truth and holiness, in the integrity of their faith in, and understanding of, Catholicism, and in the integrity of an authentic cultivation of mind, education in the technical sense.

---

23. C. S. Lewis, *The Abolition of Man*, London 1978.
24. Pope John Paul II, *The Pope Teaches. The Pope in Britain*, London 1982, 172.

CHAPTER FIVE

The Theological Formation of Seminarians

Pope St Gregory the Great remarks at the beginning of the *Pastoral Care* that since 'the government of souls is the art of arts', it is preposterous to desire to be a priest without first acquiring the necessary learning.[1] 'For who does not realise that the wounds of the mind are more hidden than the internal wounds of the body? Yet, although those who have no knowledge of the powers of drugs shrink from giving themselves out as physicians of the flesh, people who are utterly ignorant of spiritual precepts are often not afraid of professing themselves to be physicians of the heart.' Over sixteen hundred years later, a successor of St Gregory in the See of Peter stressed that the very different circumstances of our times require 'a high level of intellectual formation, such as will enable priests to proclaim, in a context like this, the changeless gospel of Christ and to make it credible to the legitimate demands of reason'.[2]

In this chapter my subject will be the theological formation of candidates for the priesthood who 'in their minds must be the same as Christ Jesus' (Phil 2:5). More precisely, it will be the issue of their appropriate and fruitful initiation into the disciplines composing the programme of theological studies by which each seminarian 'participates in the light of God's mind'.[3] My

---

1. St Gregory the Great, *Pastoral Care*, translated and annotated by Henry Davis SJ, Ancient Christian Writers Series (Westminster Maryland: 1950), 51; see *Patrologia Latina*, LXXVII, 13-128. This chapter began as a paper delivered at an international conference on the formation of priests in Venice in 1996.
2. Pope John Paul II, *Pastores Dabo Vobis*, Apostolic Exhortation on the Formation of Priests, 1992, art 51.
3. Ibid., 51.

concern will not simply be the depth of study and the amount of time that is appropriate in the teaching of scripture, dogma, morality and church history, but rather the theological vision inspiring and guiding the whole programme of studies.

In order to achieve this goal it will first be appropriate to state the core of Christian faith and to highlight, however briefly, its uniqueness and divine originality. In the second, I will discuss briefly seven component aspects of that divine love communicated to humankind and history through the crucified and glorified Christ. Only explicit reference to the practical implications of these will provide the authentic setting and proper inspiration for theological education. In the third section, the fundamental challenge to theology posed by the originality of such a trinitarian, crucified and glorified Love will be considered: theology must measure itself against its revealed standard and recognise the links it has with the other areas of Christian life and priestly formation. Finally, we will attempt to sketch the most elementary outline of a three-year course corresponding to the theo-logic now developed.

I. The Total Newness of Christianity

In order to consider theology at all it is first necessary to ask what constitutes Christian faith today. Theology is after all but a derivative of this faith, together with its hope and charity, seeking understanding, according to the classical definition. In the consideration of this question of what constitutes faith today a renowned theologian[4] turns at once to St Paul for the answer. The classic passage he opens is the one in Romans 10:9-10, 'If your lips confess that Jesus is Lord, and if you believe in your heart that God raised him from the dead, then you will be saved. By believing from the heart you are made righteous; by confessing with your lips you are saved.' The parallel message is communicated also in John. It is in fact clearly formulated in First John and in the Johannine literature in general. The *locus classicus* is 1 Jn 4:8-10:

4. J. Ratzinger, *Principles of Catholic Theology,* San Francisco 1987, 15f.

God is love.
God's love for us was revealed
when God sent into the world his only Son
so that we could have life through him;
this is the love I mean:
not our love for God,
but God's love for us when he sent his Son
to be the sacrifice that takes our sins away.

The text is one of those masterpieces of Johannine brevity which carry a content of even more surprising fullness. The first element is the 'definition' of God as it were. 'God is love' has a clear trinitarian content as the rest of the text clearly indicates. This text succinctly summarises the economy of God's action in the world and in history, culminating in the mission of the Son to give life to us. It is this revelation that enables us to grasp that God is this self-sacrificing love that squanders itself for us and for the life of the world (Jn 6: 51).

The truth is that it is easy to say, 'God is love', and mean very little by the statement. It is the fact of the incarnation of the Son of the Father and his becoming obedient unto death to the extent of his abandonment on the cross in order 'to gather together in unity the scattered children of God' (Jn 11:52), that puts flesh and blood on that central statement of Christian faith in the New Testament. Jesus crucified and forsaken unites humankind to the Father and restores the lost unity of the human family. He is therefore both the interpreter and the final self-exegesis of the Trinity to us, as well as the key to the mystery of human existence.[5]

John sets the Father's love and 'our love for God' in opposition, not simply for the sake of effect but rather to highlight the selfless and boundless freedom of the divine initiative: nothing in us attracted or motivated the divine love to act in such an

5. See *Gaudium et spes*, 22: 'In fact, it is only in the mystery of the Word incarnate that light is shed on the mystery of humankind.' Translation from Norman P. Tanner, SJ, *Decrees of the Ecumenical Councils*, II, London and Washington DC 1990, 1081.

unheard of and astounding fashion for us. In fact, there is in God something greater than God, so to speak, something not measurable by any human criterion whatsoever. It is this reality which fascinates and attracts our love as a response. It is this *magis* that is the driving force in the whole plan of God.

Perhaps a hymn from the *Liturgy of the Hours* captures this elusive but vital aspect of divinity which John so masterfully highlights. The hymn, taken from First Vespers for the Ascension, makes the shocking claim, using the two verbs '*vincere*' and '*cogere*', that the Christ was conquered (*sic*) and forced (*sic*) to show mercy and endure the abandonment (see Mt 27:46; Mk 15:34).[6] The hymn speaks for itself: *Quae te vicit clementia / ut ferres nostra crimina?[...] Ipsa te cogat pietas.* 'What was that mercy that conquered you to the point that you carried our crimes?' And the answer comes, 'It was your loving kindness.'[7] The object of praise in this hymn is the staggering love of the Saviour. More significantly, it presents this love as more godly than God, indeed as stronger than God, as more powerful than God since it 'conquers' God and 'pushes' God! It is this reality which is earlier, older and more divine than anything that we are accustomed to say of God!

In God there is something that is 'older' than his sovereignty and invincibility, and it is precisely this older reality which is the newness that grounds and expresses the originality of God. We encounter this originality in his redeeming love: God does not remain in his heaven, nor does one exhaust his reality with the appellation of Unmoved Mover. God dares to enter into the play of our history, to dirty his hands with us, to take on what is ours, to carry what is ours, to become one of us. It is this newness of God which is, according to this

---

6. See G. Rossé, *Il grido di Gesù in Croce. Una panoramica esegetica e teologica*, Rome 1984, for an elaborate treatment of the Markan and Matthaen texts on the exegetical and theological levels.

7. The Latin word *pietas* has a rich variety of meanings such as 'dutifulness', 'desire to carry out the wishes of a beloved and respected person', 'grateful and affectionate dispositions towards someone'.

hymn, what is older in God, for he is compelled and forced by his own love for the sake of love.[8]

Here we realise that all our categories break down under the weight of what is revealed, as inadequate to speak about their subject as narrow pipes are to carry the waters of the mountain torrent. That is why St Paul prays for the Ephesians so that they might come to the knowledge of the love of Christ which surpasses all knowing (3:19). God is precisely this trinitarian, crucified and glorified love that is so great that none greater can be thought.[9] It is this 'greater' that is the originality of Christianity, its 'ever-more'[10] quality that attracts and renews.

God the Holy Trinity is the self-squandering love that gathers up the whole world into unity. This is the 'light that shines in the dark, a light that darkness could not overpower' (Jn 1: 8). Here is the light for our existence, the divine 'clarity' which 'enlightens all men' (1:9) so that this glory of Christ shines out, 'the glory that is his as the only Son of the Father, full of grace and truth' (1: 14). To catch even a glimpse of that glory is to be drawn into the mystery of God the Holy Trinity and to be readied for the priestly ministry. It is enough to think of those striking opening verses of First John (1:1-4), with their sequence of 'sense verbs', to realise both the fountainhead of the apostolic experience and the joyful commitment to the task of making this known to others.

8. K. Hemmerle, 'Das Neue ist älter. Hans Urs von Balthasar und die neue Orientierung der Theologie', *Ausgewählten Schriften*, Band 2, Freiburg 1996, 203, 'In Gott ist etwas älter als seine Unbezwingbarkeit und Unbesieglichkeit, und dieses Ältere ist zugleich das, was die Neuigkeit, das Neue Gottes trägt und ausmacht. Diesem Neuen begegnen wir in seiner erlösenden Liebe: Gott bleibt nicht in seinem Himmel, Gott ershöpft sich nicht darin, unbeweglicher Beweger zu sein. Gott gibt sich selbst hinein in das Spiel unserer Geschichte, er macht sich sozusagen die Hände schmutzig mit uns, er nimmt das Unsere an, trägt uns, wird einer von uns. Diese Neuigkeit Gottes ist nach Ausweis des Hymnus das Ältere in Gott; denn er ist zur Liebe von seiner eigenen Liebe genötigt und gezwungen.' The translation is my own.
9. St Anselm, *Proslogion*, 3.
10. See Hanspeter Heinz, *Der Gott des Je-mehr. Der christologische Ansatz Hans Urs von Balthasar*, Frankfurt 1975, passim.

In his own distinctive way, Paul brings out this same reality of the light in his Letter to the Philippians. In chapter two he sets forth the mystery of Christ showing the divine design for history, focusing on the *kenosis* of the Son. In the following chapter he states his own response to the total mystery of Christ: 'All I want is to know Christ and the power of his resurrection and to share his sufferings by reproducing the pattern of his death' (3:11). Finally, he exhorts the Christians to imitate and follow his way and witness (3:17-21).

II. A brief Phenomenology of Divine Love

This love is the core and the substance of Christianity. It illuminates the whole of existence and sheds its glorious radiance on each and every aspect of daily life (see 2 Cor 4:6). It therefore illuminates the intellectual elaboration of that one light, namely, 'theology'. As von Balthasar stresses, 'What theology needs is to be steeped anew in the very heart of the love mystery of scripture, and to be remoulded by the force it exerts.'[11] But not only theology, for the truth is that theology is only one aspect of that light's reality. In the New Testament, I detect six other aspects besides the formally theological one! These seven aspects may be likened to the seven colours of the rainbow. Just as when a ray of light is passed through a prism and breaks into its seven component colours, so too the light of God's self-communication by which we know him as love has seven aspects which bathe the whole of life and all its components.

The reason for this section in this reflection is quite simple: since theology is only one of what would appear to be seven constituent colours of the Light, God who is love, it becomes stilted and unreal when it is not clearly connected with the whole life of the seminarian. It is notorious in fact how little theology and spirituality actually seem to connect and nourish each other in spite of the substantial presence of both in the cur-

11. Hans Urs von Balthasar, *Word and Revelation*, vol I, translated by A. V. Littledale with the co-operation of Alexander Dru, New York 1964, 162.

riculum of theological faculties and seminaries. The inevitable result of this failure is that seminarians often have but little esteem for their theological studies because these studies seem to have so little to do with daily living in the seminary and beyond. Once ordained and into ministry, the gap between theology and ministry may become even more glaring. The result is frequently the abandonment of serious reading and reflection on the part of many.

What is this sevenfold form of love? In the first place, divine love makes believers ready and able to share their goods both spiritual and material. This interchange of goods contributes to the formation of an authentic communion of persons. An instance of such communion is to be seen in the Acts. We are told there that 'no one was ever in want, as all those who owned land or houses would sell them, and bring the money from them to present it to the apostles; it was then distributed to any members who might be in need' (4:34-5). This raises the question for all Christians: how do we possess, how do we give? Are we truly brothers and sisters for each other? The seminarian of today is called to be a man of communion, not because he is preparing for priestly ministry, but primarily in order to be an authentic Christian. The great threat is individualism which can only be countered by another style of life, where solidarity lived out among the students creates an ethos of communion.

Secondly, love wants to give and to radiate. St Thomas wrote that 'goodness is self-donating.'[12] According to Pope Paul VI, the only proof that a person has heard the gospel is the desire to communicate it to others. Here we are face to face with the need to witness and to live the manifold dialogue called for by the church at the Council and since. Seminaries can be expected to radiate something of that witness. It is this witness that manifests itself in pastoral and missionary work: such activities are the overflow of the love of God flooding our hearts (see Rom 5:5) and going out to others. In the first Christian community in

---

12. St Thomas, *Summa Theologica*, I, Q.5, 4 ad 2: *bonum dicitur diffusivum sui esse, eo modo quo finis dicitur movere.*

Jerusalem the life of love reached out in practical ways to the hungry so that 'they [the Christians] were looked up to by everyone' (Acts 2:47).

Thirdly, love both elevates and plumbs the depths. This aspect of love summons up the whole area of prayer and spirituality. It calls for a life lived from scripture, nourished by the sacraments, patterned on Jesus. Faith then becomes the fountainhead of our daily living so that we 'love as Christ loved us, giving himself up in our place' (Eph 5:2). The *Decree on Priestly Formation* stresses the danger of superficiality in the spiritual formation of candidates,[13] while *Pastores Dabo Vobis* draws out the implications even more fully.[14]

Fourthly, love creates a family atmosphere. Here the interplay of work and relaxation, of sport and entertainment come into view. Christian revelation highlights the dignity of the whole person and the consequent duty to take appropriate care of one's health. Recreation and the use of free time should reflect the choice of God at the basis of the seminarian's life and calling. The quality of the food we eat and our care of those who are sick need careful attention. Many a seminary rector will tell of his anxiety at the unusual eating habits of some students and the need to inculcate a proper but serene attitude to promote the health of both the individual and the whole seminary community, students and staff.

Fifthly, love harmonises, and this harmony raises the matter of our immediate surroundings. God is that glory-beauty whose light 'has shone in our minds' (2 Cor 4:6) and we are temples of his Holy Spirit (1 Cor 6:19). It is imperative therefore that we dress this temple with taste and reverence, and that we furnish and decorate our dwellings with care for harmony and beauty. This applies of course in a particular way to the manner in which we keep the seminary building, its chapel and other oratories.

Sixthly, love longs to see and to understand. Whoever loves

13. *Optatam Totius*, 13-8.
14. *Pastores Dabo Vobis*, sections 45-50.

has eyes, wrote Thomas Aquinas. Love longs to study, to ponder and to treasure (see Luke 2:19, 51) so as to attain to that 'tasting knowledge' which is wisdom. The outcome of such a love-inspired theology is a wisdom that is both experienced and lived. All Christians need to develop a sympathetic and still discerning involvement with the world. This need is even more pressing in the case of those preparing to be shepherds of souls in the modern world. I will return to this aspect of love shortly.

Finally, love constructs bonds among all those united by its embrace. Communication among the seminarians is of great importance. In particular they learn the art of sharing with discretion significant experiences in order to build up that kind of family that answers the high-priestly prayer of Jesus (see Jn 17:21f). The communication of the news in God's family is vital since it builds the whole community increasingly into one. The use of the various mass media has greatly facilitated this process. Do not seminarians today need to be masters of the various means of communication and, on a personal level, be adept at keeping contact with people by letter, phone-call, e-mail and texting? In that way they acquire the skills necessary to be able to construct 'the net of God' (Pope John Paul II).

The light of trinitarian, crucified and glorified God-Love thus sheds its kindly radiance over the whole spectrum of our concrete daily life. In that way it is not only the source and origin of all theology but also the key to the how of seminary living. It ensouls the community by a sharing of material and spiritual goods, inspires the pastoral outreach from a sound basis in concrete witness so that seminarians can tell others about what they have heard and seen and touched with their hands (see 1 John 1: 2), and provides the substance of spirituality in word, sacrament, and cross. It attends to health of soul and body. It highlights the importance of order and harmony in dress, decoration and buildings, and it focuses on the importance of communications on all levels in the church. And from the perspective of this study we suggest that all of these aspects, providing as they do a kind of phenomenology of revealed and incarnated love, also provide fresh data for theology.[15]

III. THE TOTAL NEWNESS (ST IRENAEUS) OF CHRISTIANITY

Christian revelation, then, puts an extraordinary life before us. In the process 'it opens up vistas closed to human reason'.[16] It not only communicates the trinitarian life to humankind, drawing humankind into this realm as its proper *Lebensraum*, but also manifests the true meaning and purpose of person and society, the world and history itself.

From the beginning of the church's history, the divine freshness of this mystery was highlighted. Writing about AD 124, the anonymous author of *The Letter to Diognetus* compares the presence of the Body of Christians in the Empire with the presence of the soul in the body: they are the very life-principle of the Empire that persecutes them. 'The thing they guard so jealously is no product of mortal thinking, and what has been committed to them is the stewardship of no human mysteries. The Almighty himself, the Creator of the universe, the God whom no eye can discern, has sent down his very own Truth from heaven, his own holy and incomprehensible Word, to plant it among men and ground it in their hearts.'[17] A short while later another great thinker of the early church, St Irenaeus of Lyons (+c AD 210), wrote the famous line, *Christus omnem novitatem attulit, seipsum afferens qui fuerat annuntiatus*[18] (Christ brought total newness by bringing himself who had been foretold).

The supreme challenge to any theology today is not to be un-

15. See H. Blaumeiser, 'Il seminario come communita di discepoli', in Gen's *Rivista di vita ecclesiale*, Roma, 4/5(1989), 132-8; see John McIntyre, *The Shape of Christology* (Edinburgh: 1998), section entitled 'What is given in Christology?' for a fascinating discussion of the issue of what constitutes the data of an area in theology, in this case Christology, 3-24.

16. *GS*, 24.

17. Maxwell Staniforth, editor, *Early Christian Writing*, London 1968, 178.

18. St Irenaeus, *Against the Heresies*, IV, 31, 4, as quoted by von Balthasar in *The Glory of the Lord*, vol II, Edinburgh 1984, 85.

faithful or inadvertent to that divine originality of Love which makes Christianity always old yet always new, and does so in such a way that what is new in God is what is older. Above all else, the guiding hermeneutic of the crucified and forsaken Christ must be placed at the centre of the theology programme. *The Catechism of the Catholic Church* stresses the point in these terms: 'The paschal mystery of Christ's cross and resurrection stands at the centre of the good news that the apostles, and the church following them, are to proclaim to the world.' This mystery, however, gives access to the other central mystery of faith. As the *Catechism* states, '[the] mystery of the Most Holy Trinity is the central mystery of Christian faith and life. It is the mystery of God in himself. It is therefore the source of all the other mysteries of faith, the light that enlightens them. It is the most fundamental and essential teaching in the "hierarchy of the truths of faith".'[19]

1. The Return to the Centre

This century has been characterised by the movement of *ressourcement* in theology. The renewals in biblical and patristic studies, in liturgical and historical theology have opened up again the riches of the faith. The *épanouissement* of these renewals was the Council where the fruits of more than a century of sustained research into the newly rediscovered 'Great Tradition' appeared. It is interesting in this context to note that the *Decree on the Formation of Priests* affirms unequivocally the validity of the recovered resources. To take but one example, the Council states, 'Dogmatic theology should be so arranged that the biblical themes are presented first. Students should be shown what the Fathers of the Eastern and Western church contributed to the fruitful transmission and illumination of the individual truths of revelation, and also the later history of dogma and its general relationship to the history of the church.'[20]

However, it is not only – not even primarily – by a return to

---

19. *Catechism of the Catholic Church*, Dublin 1994, sections 571, and 234.
20. *OT*, 16.

the sources that the renewal of dogma will be accomplished. This renewal must rather turn to the centre[21] in order to produce a theology from the centre, that is, from the heart of the Christian mystery. '[T]heology should be taught in such a way that students will accurately draw Catholic doctrine from divine revelation...'[22]

Asserted very powerfully in this conciliar statement is the principle that all doctrine flows out of the Christian mystery. Here is the light for theology. Von Balthasar, it seems, gets to the heart of the matter when he writes:

> Dogmas which we now know only from the outside, as the content of the faith, and which have mostly been presented to us as such in catechism and from the pulpit, we must try to see from within again as the manifestation of the one, single, indivisible truth of God. Supposing that this truth has presented itself to us as the eternal love which surprises us and lays its claims on us temporal creatures, will not the basic articulations of the so-called Christian 'doctrine' – Trinity, incarnation, cross and resurrection, church and eucharist – become the immediate radiations of the glowing core of this truth? How should God, the One and Absolute, be eternal love, if he were not triune? And how should God be absolute love, if he did not prove this being love to the end in the cross and eucharist for the life of the world, which he created out of love, and if he did not take the world up, in church and resurrection, into the eternally moved rest of the exchange of love? Dogmas must be nothing other than aspects of the love which manifests itself and yet remains mystery within revelation. If they are no longer this, then gnosis has triumphed over love, and human reason has conquered God.[23]

Since all dogmas are contained in this one Great Dogma –

21. See Hans Urs von Balthasar, *Convergences. To the Source of the Christian Mystery*, San Francisco 1983, translated by E. A. Nelson, passim.
22. *OT*, 16.
23. Von Balthasar, *Convergences. To the Source of the Christian Mystery*, passim.

'God is love' (1 Jn 4:8, 16) – they must be presented in such a way
that the minds of students perceive this derivation clearly. All
the truths of faith unfold from this glowing centre and refold
again into the same inexhaustible matrix. This dynamic of unfolding and refolding, however, needs to be brought out with
clarity so that the divine vitality of the mystery of faith is both
highlighted by the professors and understood by the students.

This has striking relevance for the various tracts of theology.
In fact, these tracts and courses, it seems to me, must needs be
designed in view of this *master principle* of unity which is the
hermeneutic of all dogma and of each dogma and insight.
'Theology can only perform its task by circular repetitions of
that which is ever-greater. Parcelling it out in isolated individual
tracts is its certain death.'[24] Perhaps we are now close to the
heart of the malaise affecting much theology heretofore: the
many tracts were simply disconnected from one another and
also from the centre. Now this would seem to be in conflict with
the church's teaching in Vatican I highlighting that most fruitful
understanding of the revealed mysteries as the very purpose of
theological formation and study, and which is to be reached by
means of, among others, the interconnection of the mysteries
among themselves.[25]

Two specific instances may perhaps illustrate the point
which is so crucial. Karl Rahner has written on the negative effect of the separation of the two tracts on God in the regular
theology courses of candidates for the priesthood over the recent centuries.[26] The tract *De Deo Uno* dealt in general with the

---

24. Idem, *Theologik*, I, Einsiedeln 1985, viii; this text is quoted in John
Saward, *The Mysteries of March*, London 1990, xvii.
25. *DS* 3016: 'If reason, illuminated by faith, inquires earnestly, piously,
and soberly, it attains, by God's grace (*Deo dante*), a certain understanding of the mysteries, which is most fruitful, both by analogy with the
things it knows naturally, and from the connection of the mysteries with
one another (*e mysteriorum ipsorum nexu inter se*) and with man's ultimate
end.' The translation is from J. Saward, *The Mysteries of March*, 152.
26. K. Rahner, 'Remarks on the dogmatic treatise "De Trinitate",'
Theological Investigations, IV, London 1966, 77-102. Translation by Kevin
Smyth.

God of natural theology, while the *De Deo Trino* presented a speculative account of the Holy Trinity in the light of the so-called psychological analogy. The net result was a serious loss of substance in the student's perception of the Christian mystery and the conviction that theology was abstract rather than life-giving.

The second instance concerns the standard treatise on the theology of grace in recent centuries. Based on scripture, and having particular recourse to the Fathers, John Henry Newman delivered his lectures on the doctrine of justification and grace in 1837. The Anglican Newman set out to develop a more 'theological theology' of grace by advancing beyond the positions then current in both popular Romanism and popular Protestantism. The result was a quality of theology which Louis Bouyer has described as 'soaring above the unsatisfying aridities of textbook theology'. Newman found 'in the wealth of Catholic tradition the spirit that might have given those original Protestants complete satisfaction, fulfilling their aspirations and removing all risk of their falling into heresy or schism'.[27] The central concern of theology, then, is to unite and connect, not divide and fragmentise.

2. Theology and Life

The second area of concern to the recent magisterium of the church on theological formation of future priests addresses the necessary bonding of theology and spirituality. The church wants 'theology ... taught in such a way that students ... will nourish their own spiritual lives with it.'[28] There is a crying need to connect *sacra doctrina* with *sancta vita*. The separation of the two has done incalculable damage to the church over the past millennium. Perhaps von Balthasar is again closer to the mark when he writes: 'In the whole history of Catholic theology there is hardly anything that is less noticed, yet more deserving of

27. L. Bouyer, *Newman His Life and Spirituality*, London 1958, translated by J. Lewis May, 171.
28. *OT*, 16.

notice, than the fact that, since the great period of scholasticism, there have been few theologians who were saints.'[29] The net result of this separation of thinking and living in the church has been extremely damaging to both theology and spirituality.

> It has sapped the vital force of the church of today and the credibility of her preaching of eternal truth ... [The faithful] long to discover the living organism of the church's doctrine, rather than a strange anatomical dissection: on the one hand, the bones without the flesh, 'traditional theology'; on the other, the flesh without bones, that very pious literature that serves up a compound of asceticism, mysticism, spirituality and rhetoric, a porridge that, in the end, becomes indigestible through lack of substance.[30]

It is worth remembering that 'spirituality' in its popular connotation today does not seem to embrace the whole of life. The Gospel addresses the whole of our lives since the Triune God of love sheds his light on every sector of human and historical existence. This was the burden of the section above on the aspects of the light and the phenomenology of love. Since theology is only *one* of those seven colours, it can attain its specific hue only when the other six are also present. In brief, it is dangerous in the extreme to study the revealed word, without first living by that same word. The scriptures love to characterise the word as 'the Word of Life' (Phil 2:16), a word requiring obedience (Lk 1:38; 2:19, 51; Mt 7:24-7; Lk 8:21; Rom 2:13; James 1:21-4; 1 Jn 3:17f). Jesus promises, 'If anyone loves me he will keep my word, and my Father will love him, and we shall come to him and make our home in him'(Jn 14:23). And again, 'Anybody who receives my commandments and keeps them will be one who loves me; and anybody who loves me will be loved by my Father, and I shall love him and show myself to him' (Jn 14:21).

29. Von Balthasar, *Word and Redemption*, vol 2, New York 1965, 49.
30. *Ibid.*, 65.

3. The Unity of Philosophy and Theology

'In the revision of ecclesiastical studies, the first object in view must be a better integration of philosophy and theology.' This is the policy of the Council.[31] In early Christianity the unity of philosophy and theology is the norm. Justin the Martyr is convinced that 'gospel and philosophy do not face the believer with a choice of alternatives, nor are they complementary aspects of truth which the thinker would have to weld into the complete truth; in his conception, the *Logos* of the gospel is rather the same word of the same God as the *logos spermatikos* of philosophy, but at a later state of its manifestation in history.'[32] The gospel did not reject all philosophy but rather absorbed the life of the mind into the overflowing pleroma of the revelation of the infinite Word of God. The seeking of the human spirit was gathered up into the drawing of the Father who draws towards his incarnate Son[33] (see Jn 6:44). Pope John Paul wished to refresh our memory when in the very first words of his last encyclical, *Fides et Ratio*, he could write: 'Faith and reason are like two wings on which the human spirit rises to the contemplation of truth – in a word, to know himself – so that, by knowing and loving God, men and women may also come to the fullness of truth about themselves (cf Ex 33:18 ; Ps 27:8-9 ; 63:2-3 ; Jn 14:8 ; 1 Jn 3:2).'

In the first centuries the gospel convincingly addressed the abiding questions. Joseph Ratzinger has effectively shown that 'both faith and philosophy confront the primordial question which death addresses to man ... Death, the one question which it is impossible to ignore forever, is thus a metaphysical thorn lodged in man's being.'[34] This happy rapport of revelation and philosophy, however, has been greatly upset in recent centuries.

---

31. *OT*, 14.

32. Eric Voegelin, 'The Gospel and History', in *Published Essays 1966-1985*, Baton Rouge and London 1990, 173.

33. 'The terms seeking (*zetein*) and drawing (*helkein*) do not denote two different movements but symbolise the dynamics in the tension of existence between its human and divine poles.' *Ibid.*, 183.

34. J. Ratzinger, *The Nature and Mission of Theology*, San Francisco 1995, translated by Adrain Walker, 23.

First, a distinction was made between the two in such a way at the time of scholasticism that the two actually separated subsequently. Then, with the negative attitude of the Reformation towards reason, and the still more radical positions adopted by the Enlightenment with respect to faith, a scenario emerged where philosophy and theology now tend to ignore one another when they are not actually hostile.

This scenario poses a special challenge to theology which must regain its dialogue with philosophy and philosophy's search for the answers to those eternal questions which simply refuse to disappear or be banished from human consciousness. The difficulty of this enterprise, however, should not be underestimated, for among the many consequences of the separation of faith and reason 'was an ever-deeper mistrust with regard to reason itself ... It should also be borne in mind that the role of philosophy itself has changed in modern culture. From universal wisdom and learning, it has been gradually reduced to one of the many fields of human knowing; indeed in some ways it has been consigned to a wholly marginal role.'[35] While this is an issue which I cannot develop here, suffice it to say that at the very core of revelation there is the wonder of the crucified Christ who is forsaken by heaven and earth. Is not this forsaken Christ, who in his death-agony cries out 'Why?', the God of those who have no answers or who propose this forsakenness of humankind as the normal condition of humankind to be borne with a kind of heroic fortitude that in the final analysis is futile?[36]

4. Scripture: 'The Soul of all Theology'

In the method of theology envisaged by *Optatam Totius* the biblical theme is central and decisive. This is hardly any wonder in the light of *Dei Verbum*'s teaching on the nature and dignity of scripture.[37] The Council not only proposes a 'progressive'

35. *Fides et Ratio*, 45, 47.
36. See P. Coda, 'Vivere la teologia oggi' in *Trinità. Vita di Dio, Progetto dell'uomo*, Rome 1987, 74-95.
37. See *Dei Verbum*, chapter VI,'Sacred Scripture in the life of the Church'.

method (in short, from scripture to dogma) to replace the earlier 'regressive' method (from dogma to scripture). But the Council also makes it crystal clear that scripture is no mere first stage in the elaboration of a tract on dogma but an abiding, sustaining and nourishing presence throughout, just as the soul is all-pervasive of the body which it animates. Scripture has the role of animating the whole of theology in all of its branches.

The above considerations should now permit us to draw up somewhat more precise suggestions with regard to how a syllabus of theological studies appropriate to the formation of ministers of the gospel might be framed.

IV. Towards an Alternative Programme of Theology

The Son of God is God's own Theology, while the Father is the Theologian (cf. Jn 1:18). In that way, God becomes his own interpreter, since it is the Son made flesh who, in the words just referred to, interprets the Father to humankind.[38] That Son interprets the Father in the depths of suffering and in the darkness of death, even death on a cross (Phil 2:8). This light of revelation and faith is the light that must permeate the whole of theology.

For practical purposes we will assume that the foundational theology programme runs for three years or six semesters. It would be unrealistic to expect that all the various disciplines could be so tailored as to dovetail into one another. But at least dogma and scripture are two core subjects so closely related to each other that it should be possible for them to present their various tracts so as to bring out their implicit unity. In the first year, the unifying theme might perhaps best be formulated as 'Christ the mediator and fullness of all revelation.'[39] Thus, e.g., as far as dogma is concerned, the obvious topics to be treated in the first semester would be revelation, its transmission, divine inspiration and the interpretation of scripture; Christology and Trinity could be treated in the second. The synoptic gospels sug-

38. See Hans Urs von Balthasar, 'God is his own Exegete', in *Communio*, 1 (1986), 280-6.
39. See *DV* 2.

gest themselves as the most suitable topics for an introduction to exegesis, while in the second semester the focus could be on the Johannine corpus. (Against this background, moral theology might, in the first semester, take the theme of discipleship of Christ as the focus for an introduction to that discipline; the basic moral principles could be discussed in the second semester.)

The theme that suggests itself for the second year is 'the church as the sacrament of Christ'.[40] Over the course of two semesters, dogma might begin with a course in pneumatology, leading to ecclesiology and sacramental theology. (Such a context would suggest that the introduction to sacred liturgy be taken in the second semester.) Scripture might concentrate on the Pauline corpus in the first semester, Pentateuch and the Prophets in the second.

The third year would address the theme of 'the person in Christ'. Creation and original sin could in the first semester be intelligibly presented under the theme of 'the person in need of Christ'. Grace and eschatology would be treated in the second semester under the heading of 'the person living by the grace of Christ'. Exegesis would then explore the Psalms in the first semester and the Wisdom literature in the second.

Explanatory Comments

A few observations seem to be in order. First, with regard to scripture, which is 'the soul of theology', the New Testament is taught during the first three semesters while the Old Testament is taught in the remaining three. The significance of this order is to be seen in the relationship that exists in the mind of the church between scripture and the dogmatic courses in these semesters. The New Testament feeds and sustains the courses on revelation, Christology, Trinity and church. Since the theme of the first year is christological, it demands that the students immerse themselves in the gospels, the letters, and the other books of the New Testament. In that perspective the opening course on

---

40. See *LG* 1.

the synoptics might highlight their central revelational and christological themes. In that same context one should also notice the positioning of the dogmatic tract on the inspiration and interpretation of scripture: here a *doctrine* of scripture might be proposed so that the student realises from the outset the *nature* of the inspired word that has to be interpreted and transmitted.

In the second place, the dogmatic or systematic tracts are in a sequence that is determined by the principle that 'theology can only perform its task by circular repetitions of that which is ever-greater. Parcelling it out in individual isolated tracts is its certain death.'[41] Now that 'ever-greater' is presented in those early dogmatic tracts which form the core of the syllabus during the first semesters. The succeeding tracts unfold the mystery. In that way the unifying 'great dogma' of trinitarian, crucified and glorified Love enlightens the whole of the course while each tract is equidistant with every other tract from that centre. In this context one should notice the appearance of the tract on the Holy Spirit. This tract on 'the Unknown God', as the Holy Spirit has been called, prepares the mind for the next tracts on the church, the sacraments and grace.

This programme aims at the statement of the essentials in theological formation. And it does this only for the first cycle, and not for the second cycle or the pastoral year preceding ordination. That would be a subject for another study.

---

41. See n 11 above.

Index of Proper Names

Augustine, St, 29
Albert the Great, St, 13
Allers, Rudolf, 65
Ambrose, St, 77
Anselm, St, 60
Aristotle, 8
    wonder, 26
    importance of truth, 50
    conception of God, 54
Athanasius, St, 77
Aquila, Dominic A., 35, 49
Aquinas, St Thomas, 13
    faith and reason, 43
    love, 87, 89

Bacon, Francis, 14
Balthasar, Hans Urs von,
    faith and culture, 58-9
    theology and spirituality, 65-6
    dogma and scripture, 86, 92-4
Barberi, Dominic, 76
Basil, St, 40
Benedict XVI, Pope, 13
faith and reason, 82, 96
Bonaventure, 13
Bouyer, L., 46, 71, 94
Buber, Martin 65

Calvin, John, 13
Castle, E. B., 30
Chesterton, G. K., 47, 68
Clutton-Brock, Sir Arthur, 25

Coda, P., 54
Cullen, Paul, Cardinal, 79
Cyprian, St, 74

Dessain, C. S., 68
de Lubac, Henri, 16
Descartes, René, 22
Dostoyevsky, Fyodor, 15

Eliot, T. S., 51, 57

Francis, St, 62

Galileo, 44
Gregory the Great, Pope, St, 81

Heidegger, Martin 31, 65
Hemmerle, Klaus, 8, 85
Henrici, P., 62
Hogan, Pádraig, 11
Hollins, T. H. B., 20
Husserl, Edmund, 65
Hutchins, R., 27

Irenaeus, St, 16, 36, 57, 90

Joachim of Fiore, 62
John the Evangelist, St, 60, 82-3
John Paul II, Pope, 13
    faith and reason, 43, 48, 96
    faith and culture, 56, 61
    phenomenology, 65,
    on Newman, 80
    theological formation, 81, 89
Judas, 59
Julian, St, 40

Justin the Martyr, 55, 96

Ker, I., 38-40

Lewis, C. S., 10, 46, 80
Livngstone, Sir Richard, 19
Lonergan, Bernard, 16
Lubich, Chiara, 7, 10
Luther, Martin, 13

Maritain, Jacques,
    educational practice, 19-22
    social reform, 30-31
Marrou, H. I., 21
McAleese, Mary, 72
Mill, John Stuart, 31

Newman, John Henry, 11-14
    the human person, 22
    university education, 33-52
    faith and culture, 55-8, 64
    the laity, 68-80
    the theology of grace, 94
Newton, Isaac, 22

O'Donoghue, N. D., 26

Pascal, Blaise, 15, 25
Paul, St, 61, 74, 82, 85-6
Paul VI, Pope,
    witness of faith, 65, 87
    on Newman, 76
Peters, R. S., 20
Plato, 8
    importance of truth, 21, 27-8, 50
    conception of God, 54

Plotinus, 58

Rahner, Karl, 59, 93
Rublev, 58

Sartre, Jean-Paul, 31
Scheler, Max, 65
Schindler, David L., 10
Scott, Thomas, 72
Shakespeare, William, 63
Sharkey, M., 73
Socrates, 8, 27
Solzhenitsyn, Alexander, 14, 55

Veale, J., 31-2
Vloet, John van der, 61
Voegelin, Eric, 14
    Greek philosophical anthropology, 21-2
    the quest for the ground, 50
    compact community of being, 56
    faith and culture, 62-4, 96
Voltaire, 58

Walsh, D., 45-6, 79
Wiseman, Nicholas, Cardinal, 68

Zwingli, Ulrich, 13